2000

# FIELD
# EXPERIENCE

# FIELD EXPERIENCE

## A Guide to Reflective Teaching

**George J. Posner**

*Cornell University*

**Fourth Edition**

Longman *Publishers USA*

**Field Experience: A Guide to Reflective Teaching,**
**Fourth Edition**

Longman, 10 Bank Street, White Plains, N.Y. 10606

Associated companies:
Longman Group Ltd., London
Longman Cheshire Pty., Melbourne
Longman Paul Pty., Auckland
Copp Clark Longman Ltd., Toronto

Production editor: Linda W. Witzling
Editorial assistant: Matt Baker
Cover design: Tom Smith
Compositor: The Composing Room of Michigan, Inc.

**Library of Congress Cataloging-in-Publication Data**
Posner, George J.
    Field experience : a guide to reflective teaching / George J.
Posner. — 4th ed.
        p.    cm.
    Includes bibliographical references and index.
    ISBN 0-8013-1645-6
    1. Student teaching.    2. Teaching—Vocational guidance.
3. Teachers—Training of.    I. Title.
LB2157.A3P6    1996
370'.7'33—dc20                                95-21591
                                              CIP

1 2 3 4 5 6 7 8 9 10-MA-9998979695

To Adrienne, Becky, and Prema

# Contents

# Preface

*F*ield Experience is intended to help students who are engaged in teaching-related fieldwork reflect on their experiences. Whether the students' field experiences consist of tutoring someone in biology, working with a reading group, leading a 4-H group, assisting an experienced English teacher with a whole class, or taking sole responsibility for teaching a social studies class, this book will help students learn from the experience. As such, it can be used as the primary text for early field experiences or student teaching or as a supplementary text in courses with field components, such as educational psychology, methods of teaching, and introduction to elementary or secondary education.

Topics include an examination of the students' concerns and goals regarding field experiences, the use of fieldwork logs, the study of the school and the community, observation of learners, interviews with the cooperating teacher, the analysis of lessons and curricula, an examination of one's own perspective on teaching, and the use of concepts from foundations and methods courses to facilitate reflection on teaching.

This book is designed to provoke thought; it is not a text filled with facts to memorize nor is it a handbook filled with do's and don'ts. If it is to stimulate reflection, students will have to do more than read this book. They will have to respond to questions, do exercises, analyze experiences, and state personal beliefs. In order to encourage this type of active involvement, the book provides space for students to write down their responses. Some of these devices will provoke more thought than others and, therefore, require more extensive and detailed responses. Some will help students work out problems they are having, whereas others will seem irrelevant to their particular field experience. Students should feel free to focus their attention on the questions and exercises that seem most pertinent to their situation.

Although the entire book is intended for use throughout a teacher education program, certain chapters are more appropriate for certain phases of the program than others. Chapters 1 to 3 are orientation chapters and are most useful before placement in a field experience. These three chapters aid in the selection of the most appropriate positions and in the use of fieldwork logs for weekly reflection on field experiences. Chapters 4 to 11 are best used to help prepare for the field experience once the position is chosen and during the early weeks of the experience. Chapter 12 helps reflection on the field experience as it nears completion. The Epilogue at the end of Chapter 12 assumes the completion of the field experience and suggests ways of reflecting on it in order to prepare for the next experience. The Appendixes provide actual examples of student fieldwork logs and progress reports as well as several self-assessment instruments.

The book's chapter organization is intended to provide flexibility of the text for use in elementary and secondary settings and in a wide range of subject matter-specific courses. You are encouraged to use the text in whatever order is appropriate to your particular syllabus.

This new edition retains many of the features of the third edition, including the basic organization of chapters. The major addition consists of an extended and more detailed treatment of fieldwork logs. Here I have attempted to incorporate what I have learned over the past few years about how to teach students to write logs that foster reflection. New logs are included in Appendix B to illustrate these points.

# Acknowledgments

This book is in some ways a collage of ideas relevant to field experience in teaching. Although each chapter reveals the influence of many people and their writings, most chapters reflect the influence of one or two principal pieces of work.

The dominant influence on Chapter 1 was Joseph Schwab's notion of "commonplaces" in his 1971 *School Review* article, "The Practical: Translation into Curriculum." Chapter 2 has two sources: M. Cohen's master's thesis at Ohio State University, "A Factor Analytic Study of Elementary School Student Teacher Concerns," as reported in Andrew Schwebel et al. in *The Student Teacher Handbook* (Barnes and Noble, 1979), and Janet Sitter's dissertation from Michigan State University entitled "The Student Teaching Experience from the Perspective of the Student Teacher." Chapter 3 is based on Carl Grant and Ken Zeichner's "On Becoming a Reflective Teacher" from the book edited by Carl Grant entitled *Preparing for Reflective Teaching: A Book of Readings* (Allyn and Bacon, 1984).

The exercises in Chapter 4 were inspired by books such as *Teaching Is . . .* by Merrill Harmin and Tom Gregory (SRA, 1974). Chapter 5 is based on many sources, including Tom Good and Jere Brophy's *Educational Psychology: A Realistic Approach*, 2nd ed. (Holt, Rinehart and Winston, 1977), and Michael Young's *Knowledge and Control* (Collier-Macmillan, 1971). However, the basic structure of the chapter and the issues addressed is based on Ann Berlak and Harold Berlak's *Dilemmas of Schooling* (Methuen, 1981).

Chapter 6 uses ideas from Doug Roberts's "Developing the Concept of 'Curriculum Emphasis'" in *Science Education* (1982), and ideas of Ed Smith and Neil Sendelbach presented in "The Programme, the Plans and the Activities of the Classroom: The Demands of Activity-based Science," a chapter in *Innovation in the Science Curriculum*, edited by John Olson (Nichols, 1982).

Chapter 7 draws on research carried out by Ken Zeichner and Bob Tabachnick at the University of Wisconsin at Madison (based on Berlak's work). Chapters 8 through 11 derive from Dan Lortie's *Schoolteacher* (University of Chicago Press, 1975), Willard Waller's *The Sociology of Teaching* (John Wiley and Sons, 1932), and Rob A. Walker and Clem Adelman's *A Guide to Classroom Observation* (Methuen, 1975).

Chapter 12 is developed out of my own work with students at Cornell in a field-based course on teaching.

Beyond these specific contributions, the general orientation of the book derives from Ann Berlak and Harold Berlak's *Dilemmas of Schooling,* the many articles and papers on the student-teaching experience, and reflective teaching by Ken Zeichner and company (including Bob Tabachnick and Carl Grant) then at the University of Wisconsin-Madison.

In addition to these major sources, criticisms by the following of earlier drafts have provided valuable help: Ken Zeichner and some of his students at Wisconsin; Bill Schubert and his students at the University of Illinois, Chicago; Richard Duschel at the University of Pittsburgh; Ken Strike, Deborah Trumbull, and Joan Egner at Cornell; Jeff Dean and his colleagues and students at SUC-Oneonta; the faculty and students at Mansfield University; and Al Rudnitsky and his students at Smith College.

And finally, I acknowledge the contribution of the reviewers of the fourth edition:

Patricia E. Baker, State University of New York, Brockport

Jack Burtch, Slippery Rock University

Ann Croissant, Azusa Pacific University

Barbara Foulks, Radford University

Deborah Gartland, Towson State University

Mary Ann McConnell-Fodor, Xavier University

Rebecca Mills, University of Nevada, Las Vegas

William R. Norris, Southern Illinois University, Carbondale

Sarah A. Spence, Wright State University

# FIELD
# EXPERIENCE

part **I**

# Orientation

# chapter 1

# Types of Field Experience

The one indispensable part of any teacher preparation program is field experience. Student teaching can be considered a special type of field experience. It is so special that it is given a specific name and preferred status within preservice programs. In certain respects, however, all field experiences are similar. In this chapter we will discuss some common features of all preservice field experiences. These common features will serve us in subsequent chapters as a map on which to locate the concerns, goals, and issues faced by all students about to begin such experiences.

## COMMON FEATURES

All teaching situations have four features in common.[1] Although these four features may seem too obvious to mention or simply appear to reflect common sense, they will be useful reference points. First, almost by definition, a teaching situation must include a *teacher* or teachers of some sort. (The term *teaching agent* could be used to include texts or machines that teach, such as programmed instruction.) Second, there is at least one *learner* (termed *pupil* or *student,* depending on how old or how serious about learning the person is). Third, there is some *subject matter* or material that the teacher shares with, presents to, or negotiates with the learner; that is, there is something that the teacher teaches (the "stuff" of teaching), be it academic knowledge, personal feelings, or technical skills.

There is always a danger that a teaching situation will lack the necessary balance of these three features. When teaching ignores the learner, there is a tendency to be autocratic; when it ignores the teacher, it tends to be laissez-faire; when it ignores the subject matter, it is typically empty.

This "triad"[2] occurs within the fourth feature of a teaching situation—a social and physical *context* consisting of rules, facilities, values, expectations, and personal backgrounds, which act as resources, constraints, and direct influences on teaching and learning. Figure 1.1 summarizes these features.

When we think of teachers, learners, subject matter, and context, many issues come to mind. Each of these features serves as a category of issues for a discussion about educational topics. In fact, if these four features are truly comprehensive, we would expect all educational issues to fall into one or more of these categories.

## Teachers

When we consider the teacher, we are addressing issues such as the following:

- The kind of person the teacher should be
- The proper role of the teacher
- The reasons people choose teaching as a career and stay in or leave the profession
- The reasons teachers burn out or remain fresh
- The tasks teachers face in classrooms

## Learners

In a sense, we are and will always be learners, regardless of our age or position. Obviously the range of potential learners is immense, particularly if we consider not only ages but also purposes, aspirations, and backgrounds. We must also consider that this

**FIGURE 1.1**    The four common features of teaching

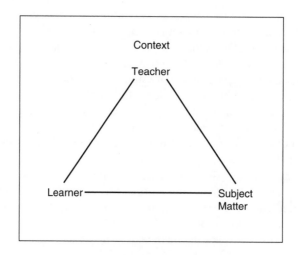

diversity greatly affects any teaching. Furthermore, there is quite a difference between teaching in a one-on-one situation and teaching a large group of diverse individuals. In one-on-one (or one-to-*small* group) situations, issues such as the following arise regarding the learner:

- What the learner already knows
- What comes easily or with difficulty
- What learners consider to be relevant
- The anxieties that must be taken into account
- The learner's future career
- What the learner is likely to find interesting, stimulating, or challenging

When teaching a group of learners, additional issues arise:

- The treatment of learners, as unique individuals or as members of categories (e.g., gifted and talented, non-college bound)
- The degree to which learners should be treated equally or differently
- Whether the fastest, the middle, or the slowest learners should be used as a reference for decisions about when to move on to new material (i.e., pacing)
- Whether the teacher should try to develop a sense of "groupness"

## Subject Matter

What teachers teach ranges from facts and concepts to thinking processes, to physical skills, to values and feelings. One issue of concern is the relative importance of each of these domains of subject matter. For example, we might question the legitimacy of using the teacher's or the learner's own feelings as subject matter for instruction. Or, we might try to decide whether to regard subject matter as truths to be learned or to emphasize how truth is reached.

Another important issue concerns the fact that time is a very scarce commodity. We simply do not have the time to teach everything as completely as desired. Therefore, we always seem to be faced with the "breadth versus depth" issue. For example, how much should we try to cover, and to what extent should we take the time to get all the students to understand the material fully? How do we reconcile these often conflicting demands for coverage and mastery?

## Context

Students and classrooms are unique places that do not change very much. They have distinctive physical and social qualities that persist from generation to generation. Philip Jackson[3] asks us to imagine entering a school at night with nobody else there and all the lights off. The smell alone would tell us where we are. The distinctive smells of cleaning fluids, chalk dust, and pencil shavings would give it away. Turning on the lights would confirm our location.

School bulletin boards may be changed but they are never discarded, the seats may be arranged but thirty of them are there to stay, the teacher's desk may have a new plant on it but there it sits, as ubiquitous as the roll-down maps, the olive drab wastebaskets, and the pencil sharpener on the window ledge.[4]

In terms of social context the classroom is also highly unique and stable. The makeup of classes and the faculty does not change drastically during the year. The conditions are almost always crowded. "Only in schools do thirty or more people spend several hours each day literally side by side. Once we leave the classroom we seldom are required to have contact with so many people for so long a time."[5] The daily schedule, types of classroom activity (e.g., seatwork, teacher demonstration), and rules (e.g., "keep your eyes on your own paper during tests") are highly uniform.

Life there [in school] resembles life in other contexts in some ways, but not all. There is, in other words, a uniqueness to the student's world. School, like church and home, is someplace special. Look where you may, you will not find another place quite like it.[6]

Context includes all that constrains, facilitates, or otherwise influences what teachers and learners do with subject matter. Context, therefore, includes the immediate physical and social environment of the classroom. But it also includes the administration of the school, parental influences, the media (especially television), laws, court decisions, governmental regulations, the backgrounds of learners and teachers, the money available to finance education, and the time available for teaching.

From a broader viewpoint, the school is one of society's most pervasive institutions and, as such, can be held responsible for any contribution it may have made to societal problems. Even if the school is not responsible for these problems, some people see it as a powerful force for reforming society.

Institutions and agencies other than schools also offer distinctive contexts that influence teaching. For example, the 4-H program, the Boy Scouts and Girl Scouts, and other youth groups may not have buildings and rooms built solely for their meetings, but their meeting places still affect them. Furthermore, youth groups operate within distinctive social contexts, often highlighted by rituals (or pledges and oaths). Some groups specify special clothing (uniforms), badges, and handbooks or manuals. Each of these aspects of the social and physical environment influences any teaching that takes place in the youth groups.

Issues derived from the contextual aspects of teaching include the following:

- The amount of input that parents should have into the program of the school or group
- The extent to which the problems facing teachers and learners are due to problems in the society at large, in the organization of schools, in the individual learner, or in the learner's family

- The extent to which the teacher or group leader can or should criticize the policies and practices of the government, the schools, the youth group or agency, or other teachers or co-workers, and the extent to which the teacher or group leaders should try to encourage such criticism by the learner
- The value of using the community at large as an educational resource

### The Four Common Features as a Whole

It would be difficult, if not impossible, to think of teaching without any one of these four features. Teaching without someone or something doing the teaching sounds absurd. Teaching without someone to teach sounds like a charade. Teaching without something to teach sounds like a waste of everybody's time. Teaching without any context sounds impossible.

Not only are all the features necessary, they are also of equal importance. These four features comprise the whole of the phenomenon we call education.[7] Any particular conception of education—whether psychological, sociological, or philosophical—provides at best one perspective of this whole, and, more typically, one perspective on one facet of the whole. Care must be exercised if we are to maintain an approach that includes the whole of teaching. Concern with maintaining our role as teachers should not blind us to the ways in which the learner learns best. Concern for covering the subject matter should not blind us to the needs of the learners. Concern for the learner's feelings should not obscure the community's expectations and the value of learning the subject matter. Neither the learner, nor the subject matter, nor the physical and social content, nor our own needs as teachers should be allowed to dominate. All features must be coordinated to achieve a balance.

The set of four features provides a map on which to locate each concern relative to the others. The set not only suggests that from each perspective we will "see *some* part of the whole . . . [but also] enables [us] to know—to some degree, at any rate— *what* part of the whole [we] will see."[8]

The common features of teaching have been expressed in somewhat abstract terms in order to make them an all-purpose way of discussing any teaching situation. Now we will try to make them more concrete.

### VARIETIES OF TEACHING SITUATIONS

No two field experiences are identical. One way to describe their differences is to refer to the four common features. We shall begin by examining the range of experiences you have already had (using the four common features) and conclude by identifying the types of experiences you are lacking.

When students in one of my classes were about to embark on an exploratory field experience, I asked for an inventory of their previous teaching experience. They responded with a very wide range of teaching situations.

1. Teaching first aid to kindergarten classes
2. Teaching balloon sculpturing to college classmates
3. Teaching long-duration hiking to a 4-H group
4. Teaching piano to a sister
5. Being a counselor at the county jail
6. Tutoring a tenth grader in history
7. Teaching a little brother to bowl
8. Teaching horseback riding to kids ages 4–15 at summer camp
9. Teaching a younger brother how to tie his shoes
10. Coaching the debating team
11. Teaching new routines and correcting moves as a sergeant in the color guard
12. Teaching a friend how to change a car's oil
13. Teaching a sister the evils of cigarette smoking (or trying to)
14. Teaching a driver-education class on drunken driving
15. Teaching backgammon to mother
16. Teaching Morse code in the navy
17. Teaching a friend to meditate

---

### EXERCISE 1.1    Inventory of Teaching Experiences

You probably have had more experience as a teacher than you realize. Maybe you took charge of a group such as scouts, 4-H, summer camp, or a club in high school. If you were responsible for what the group learned from the experience, you were a teacher. Maybe you tried to tutor someone. You might have been an official tutor. Or perhaps your friend, brother, or sister needed something explained or demonstrated. Even as a baby-sitter you might have had to explain or demonstrate something occasionally. The subject matter might have ranged from algebra to sharing toys to tying shoes. This exercise is intended to help inventory past experience as a teacher. Completing it should result in a greater awareness of previous teaching experience and a more informal basis for choosing future field experiences. Use Form 1.1 to list your teaching experiences.

**FORM 1.1**    Inventory of teaching experiences

| Experience | Subject matter | Learner's age or grade level | Context (e.g., school, camp, youth group) | Ways different from you (e.g., racial, cultural, socioeconomic) |
|---|---|---|---|---|
| 0 | Swimming | Age 7–9 | Summer camp | City kids |
| 1 | | | | |
| 2 | | | | |
| 3 | | | | |
| 4 | | | | |
| 5 | | | | |

The experiences spanned a wide range of learners, subject matter, and contexts. The learners ranged from 4-year-old children to a 40-year-old mother. The subject matter ranged from physical skills (such as shoe tying, bowling, piano playing, and changing a car's oil), to factual knowledge (such as history and Morse code), to attitudes and values (such as emotional problems of prisoners and the evils of cigarette smoking), to intellectual skills (such as debating). The contexts ranged from 1:1 tutoring and counseling to 1:30 teaching, and from educational institutions, such as schools and colleges, to youth groups and service agencies (4-H, Big Brothers, etc.), to families and friendships, and even to the armed forces.

It might be useful to examine each of your prior teaching experiences in terms of the learners, the subject matter, and the context in order to determine their range. Also consider your range of teaching experiences with people different from yourself. Use the space provided in Form 1.1 to identify these features of your experiences. How wide is your range of experiences? What types of experiences do you lack? Are any of these worth pursuing at this time?

▶

## Variety of Field Experiences

In some field-oriented courses, students have a wide choice of placements available to them. In other courses, these field placements are chosen for the student. However, whatever the situation, it is doubtful that you will have as much choice as you would like. Options are never limitless. Furthermore, rarely in life do we find ourselves in the "perfect" situation. For all these reasons, regardless of your degree of placement choice, the most productive attitude is to "bloom where you are planted," that is, to be a motivated professional in any circumstance.

One way to make certain that the environment in which you find yourself permits you to "bloom" is to look for ways in which you can adjust to the situation and in which you can adapt the placement to address your goals and concerns (see Chapter 2). Most teaching situations will allow you some flexibility.

We examine variety in field experiences as a means of thinking about this idea of mutual adaptation as well as field placement choice.

*Teacher.* Field experiences vary greatly in the roles expected of both the teacher and of you, a student functioning as the teacher's co-worker. At one extreme, the field placement might offer you the rather limited but frequently profitable role of observer, without your engaging in any real teaching. At the other extreme, you might find yourself in the more intensive role of teacher-in-charge, without much contact with other adults. Between these two extremes is the role of teacher's aide or assistant teacher. How much autonomy you want and how active a role you want to play are two key issues you need to address in your planning. Perhaps you will be able to work out an

---

The reader will notice arrows like the one above used throughout the text. They indicate that a reader response is expected.

arrangement by which you begin as an observer and gradually increase your teaching responsibilities as the semester progresses. This might be a good time to jot down your preferences for your field experience.

What kind of relationship with an experienced teacher do you prefer in your field placement? Do you want to teach actively? What sorts of tasks do you want to make sure that you tackle in your field experience? For example, do you want to plan lessons; deal with discipline problems; lead a discussion; give a lecture; supervise group activities; help individuals having problems; observe a variety of methods; or design, administer, or correct a test? How much help do you think you will need with each of these tasks?

*Learners.*    In general, a good guiding principle is to try to work with learners whose backgrounds are different from your own. The more you learn about other people and ways to teach them, the more versatile a teacher you will become. One key issue to address is the age of the learners with whom you would like to work. Depending on the opportunities available, the learners could conceivably range from 3-year-olds (e.g., in a day-care facility) to elderly people (e.g., in a nursing home). Besides age, there are other characteristics to consider when selecting a field placement or making the most of the field site in which you are placed. You might have a particular interest in working with learners who have special problems or needs (e.g., children with learning disabilities), learners with particular backgrounds (e.g., refugees), or learners with special interests and aptitudes (e.g., gifted and talented).

With what sorts of learners might you work? How old? What type of family background? Any special physical, emotional, or intellectual characteristics?

▶

*Subject Matter.*    Whether or not you realize it, you know a great deal. In fact, you probably even have substantial expertise in some areas. Take the time now to think about some of your areas of expertise. Consider not only your knowledge in academic subjects (e.g., your major), but also skills, such as athletics, computing, writing, arts and crafts, photography, drawing, music, and theater. This is a time to draw on your extracurricular activities. Don't forget that besides the obvious skills there are others we often take for granted, such as reading and speaking, using the library, and everyday survival skills (e.g., opening and maintaining a checking account). Many undergraduates assume they do not have expertise in anything until they begin to think more deeply about what they know and can do. The important point is to try to make sure that your field experience puts you in the position of teaching what you know well. Knowledge of subject matter, whatever that subject matter may be, is one prerequisite to good teaching.

What subject matter might you teach? Physical skills, attitudes, values, feelings? Facts and concepts? Intellectual skills? A mixture of these or some other type of subject matter? Might you teach academic subject matter or life skills needed to get along after schooling?

▶

*Context.* The setting in which you teach may affect the quality of your field experience. For example, teaching in a school is quite different from teaching in a youth group (like Girl Scouts). If you have a choice in the selection of your field placement, you may want to utilize your previous experiences with a particular organization by seeking a field placement in that same organization. Or, if schoolteaching is your eventual goal, you may want to get your feet wet in a classroom. Regardless of the organization, whether school or community agency, now is also the time to consider whether you would rather work one-on-one with a single learner (e.g., tutoring) or with groups of learners. Clearly, the larger the group, the less opportunity you will have to spend time with each individual. Also, management of the learners becomes a more significant issue with larger groups, although this also depends on the ability and willingness of the learners to work together cooperatively.

In what context might the teaching take place? Individual or group? In what institution? Schools? Curricular or extracurricular? What levels? Social agencies? Youth groups? Any special characteristics of the context, for example, size of group?

▶

## THE STUDENT TEACHING EXPERIENCE

Seen within this framework of teachers, learners, subject matter, and context, student teaching is a very special type of field experience.

### Learners

The learners may come from a wide range of socioeconomic and ethnic backgrounds, some of which may be quite foreign to the student teacher. The learners may also represent a broad spectrum of abilities and may range from those bordering on the mentally retarded to those considered to be geniuses. To some extent, every student-teaching experience is unique, because every learner is unique.

### Subject Matter

With the extent of their background in some school subject matter, some student teachers take that subject matter for granted, believing that others consider it significant, straightforward, interesting, and not too difficult to learn. It is important to remember, however, that most of the subject matter taught in schools is taught nowhere else and therefore is somewhat esoteric. In addition, English, social studies, science, math, art, or physical education may be easy and fun for the person who has majored in the subject but may be difficult or boring for many others. Furthermore, the learners' parents may have learned something very different in the subject when they attended school. Finally, student teachers may conceive of the subject matter in terms of just facts and concepts, but they are also teaching values and attitudes, if not explicitly then at least by example and by use of stated and unstated classroom rules. (See Chapter 5 for a more extended discussion of the "hidden curriculum.")

## Context

Of the four features, the social context and, in particular, the role of the student teacher distinguish student teaching most from all other teaching situations. The student teacher can be considered a junior partner to the cooperating teacher.[9] This role restricts both the student teacher's classroom responsibilities and opportunities for experimentation. The student teacher is not typically seen as an equal member of a teaching team, a role some professional teachers achieve; nor it the student teacher autonomous, a role most professional teachers prefer; nor is the student teacher merely an aide, because cooperating teachers typically expect the student teachers to assume increased responsibility during the term. To complicate matters further, the student teacher answers not only to the cooperating teacher but also to the college supervisor. The student teacher is still a college student and, typically, the college supervisor assigns a grade based on the supervisor's observations and the cooperating teacher's recommendations. It is unlikely that the student teacher will ever again be in a situation quite like this one. It is at the same time exciting, frustrating, and ultimately fulfilling.

## NOTES

1. See Joseph Schwab, "The Practical: Arts of Eclectic," *School Review* 79 (Aug. 1971), pp. 493–542. He terms my four common features "commonplaces."
2. David Hawkins, "I, Thou, It," *Mathematics Teaching,* Journal of the British Association of Teachers of Mathematics, No. 46 (Spring 1969).
3. Philip Jackson, *Life in Classrooms* (New York: Holt, Rinehart and Winston, 1968).
4. Ibid., pp. 6–7.
5. Ibid. p. 8.
6. Ibid., p. 9.
7. See Schwab, "The Practical," for the source of this discussion.
8. Ibid., p. 339 (italics in original).
9. Janet Sitter and Perry Lanier, "Student Teaching: A Stage in the Development of a Teacher? Or a Period of Consolidation?" Paper presented at the Annual Meeting of the American Educational Research Association, New York, March 1982.

# chapter 2

# Concerns and Personal Goals

If you are feeling a bit anxious about your field experiences, you are not alone. It may come as a surprise to learn that most of the other students about to embark on a field experience are similarly concerned. However, with some deliberate thought on the matter, you may be able to translate your anxieties and concerns into personal goals. This chapter is intended to help you make explicit the concerns that you have as you anticipate this experience and discover the feelings of other people in similar situations. Finally, this chapter will help you to identify personal goals that you might want to achieve during your field experience.

---

### EXERCISE 2.1   Expressing Concerns

Take a moment to express your primary concerns regarding your field experience. What worries you or occupies your mind about it? For example, in what ways do you feel that you will not measure up? That the experience will not be what you really want? In what ways do you feel that you will be disappointed? What really counts for your satisfaction with the experience? Make a list of these concerns in the space provided:

▶

   1.
   2.
   3.
   4.
   5.
   6.

---

## ANALYZING CONCERNS

Now we will analyze expressed concerns by using the four features of teaching (from Chapter 1) as categories of analysis. This will help stimulate further thinking about concerns.

### Learners

Who the learners are, what they are like, and how to respond to them as individuals are likely to be one area of concern. Consider the following concerns, taken from a study by Cohen and associates (1972) as reported by Schwebel et al. (1979).[1] The numbers in parentheses give the percentage of the 139 elementary school student teachers surveyed who reported these concerns as causing them moderate to very great concern.

1. Discovering and developing the potential talents of each child (76.3)
2. Presenting the work in ways that engage the students' interest (74.0)
3. Adapting assignments to the needs of the individual student (69.8)
4. Working with students who don't seem to care if they learn or not (81.3)

### Subject Matter

Teaching subject matter effectively is usually an area of concern expressed in terms of covering the material and helping learners to understand and apply it. For example:

1. Teaching students to think through problems on their own (71.2)
2. Finding sufficient time to cover the required material effectively (61.2)
3. Getting students to apply what they have learned to new problems (63.3)
4. Presenting material in ways that foster understanding (64.0)

### Context

Concern for effectively managing groups of learners involves establishing and enforcing rules, creating a climate conducive to learning, maintaining it, and restoring it constructively when necessary.[2] Such a climate is necessary to minimize the disruptive effects that one individual can have on the group and to maximize the educational benefits to all members of the group. For example:

1. Finding ways to control the students effectively (72.6)
2. Dealing with students who interfere with others' work (70.4)
3. Providing all the pupils with opportunities for class participation (55.4)
4. Dealing with classroom troublemakers (68.4)

Although these concerns are expressed in classroom terms, they apply to work within any group context (e.g., Boy Scouts). In one-to-one teaching situations such as tutoring, concerns might include:

1. Maintaining support from the teacher and the family
2. Finding a place to work with minimal distractions
3. Finding the necessary resources

## Teachers

Concern with being a competent professional typically involves being knowledgeable, being perceived as competent, and continually improving one's methods. For example:

1. Not falling into routine methods of presenting material (69.1)
2. Finding ways of keeping up with new ideas in education (57.5)
3. Achieving a good understanding of personal strengths and weaknesses with respect to teaching (56.8)

Do your expressed concerns refer primarily to the learners, the subject matter, the context, or yourself as a professional teacher? How similar are your concerns to those of others beginning a preservice field experience?
▶

## EXPRESSING GOALS

Your concerns about the upcoming field experience will greatly affect the ways in which you will benefit from it. Serious concerns can become anxieties and uncertainties that can lead to nervousness or even depression. Nobody wants that. Instead, the analysis of concerns is intended to increase the benefit of the field experience. In order for you to benefit from an examination of concerns, however, you must translate the concerns into actions. In order to do this, you have to formulate goals and plans based on your concerns.

For example, if you are concerned that you will not be able to present material in ways that engage students' interest, you might want to formulate the goal of developing the skills needed to present material in interesting ways. Or, if you are concerned that you will not be able to control students effectively, your goal might be to see if you can control students effectively. Making these goals explicit can be a productive exercise.

---

**EXERCISE 2.2    Expressing Personal Goals and Priorities**

People's goals affect their actions, expectations, and perceptions, even (and maybe especially) when they are unaware of these goals. Expressing goals makes their examination possible, thereby providing an opportunity for reassessment.

Write a few sentences describing how you expect to benefit from your field experience based on the concerns you expressed in the previous section.

▶

Now look at what you have written. You might want to compare your goals with the following generic goals:

1. To find out what teaching is really like (i.e., career exploration)
2. To see if I like teaching (i.e., exploring personal preferences)
3. To see if I can really do it (i.e., self-testing)
4. To learn some skills and modify certain habits and characteristics (i.e., training)
5. To develop my own approach or style (i.e., personal style)
6. To apply what I've learned in college to real students and to real classrooms (i.e., theory into practice)

Try considering each of your goals as a variation or specific case of one of the aforementioned six general goal types. If this matching does no violence to your goals, label your goals 1–6, according to which general goal type each represents. Try to rank order your own goals or the six goal types listed here according to how important each is to you for this particular field experience.

▶

1.
2.
3.
4.
5.
6.

What do you conclude? Do you view your field experience primarily as exploratory (goals 1 and 2), as a time to test yourself (goal 3), as a training period (goal 4), as a search for personal identity (goal 5), or as an extension of your college education (goal 6)? Where are your current priorities?

▶

---

Goals may be experienced sequentially. Early field experiences might be exploratory (goals 1 and 2) and offer an opportunity to get your feet wet, to examine teaching from the other side of the desk. The next set of field experiences might provide a chance to learn some techniques of teaching (goal 4 and perhaps 5). These intermediate field experiences can serve as a time to learn everything possible abut teaching. Courses late in the teacher education program might provide a knowledge base on which to teach (goal 6). Janet Sitter[3] found just such a progression in the "interns" she supervised. She found, however, that as they began to prepare for student teaching, their goals changed. "She no longer expressed a desire to learn all there is to know. . . . Now [that] she had been taught to teach, it was her task to go into the classroom and prove that she had learned; that she could do it."[4] That is, the students began to view student teaching less as "practice teaching" (goal 4), and more as a "proving ground" (goal 3). I mention this progression from goal 4 to goal 3 not as something student teachers should strive for, but only as an example of the way people shift goals during their teacher preparation program. Goals are tentative, not permanent.

For some students, developing a personal style or approach (goal 5) might be relevant at every level of their program. For others, it might not be seriously considered until their second or third year of regular employment, after they have survived the often traumatic first year of professional teaching. However, regardless of the pressure and intensity of the experience, goal 5 is certainly compatible with all the others and is a worthwhile ongoing goal for every field experience.

---

### EXERCISE 2.3   Setting Specific Goals

Once you have formulated personal goals to guide your field experience, it might be productive to set more specific goals. In order to do this, consider again each of the general goal types and the specific concerns you expressed earlier.

*Goal 1: To find out what teaching is really like*

Are there some specific kinds of teaching situations you would like to explore? (Refer back to your responses on page 8 in Chapter 1.)

*Learners.* Are there some specific kinds of learners about whom you want to learn? Learners with special problems? Gifted or talented learners? Particular ages? Particular ethnic backgrounds?

▶

*Subject matter.* Is there some particular subject matter you want to try teaching? A particular school subject? A sport? Do you have some specialty you want to try?

▶

*Context.* Are there any contexts that you want to explore? Particular youth groups or social agencies? Particular size groups? Team teaching? Open classrooms? Communities with special characteristics?

▶

*Teacher.* Would you like to work with or under a particular type of teacher? One with a certain philosophy or approach? One with a special type of training or background? A particular ethnic background?

▶

### Goal 2: To see if you really like teaching

Are there some specific types of teaching activities you want to try? These might include leading a discussion, giving a lecture, setting up a role play, one-to-one tutoring, helping a child with personal problems, discussing a controversial issue with a class, dealing with a disruptive child, assigning grades, meeting with a parent, designing and teaching a unit or a lesson, setting up and then teaching a laboratory lesson, or doing a demonstration.

▶

### Goal 3: To see if you can really do it

To whom do you want to prove yourself? To yourself? To a group of learners? To your college supervisor? To parents? To the cooperating teacher? To aides? Do you want to "lead" and be recognized as "the leader"? Be recognized by whom?

▶

For many teachers in training, when others recognize their leadership, they report "feeling like a teacher."[5] Developing a teacher identity plays an important role in proving oneself.[6]

### Goal 4: To learn some skills and modify certain habits and characteristics

What particular skills do you want to learn? What instructional techniques?

▶

Your goals may derive from what you regard as the keys to successful teaching. For example, most student teachers attribute successful teaching either to general good planning or to well-executed lessons, although some also specify "challenging" or "interesting" lessons, those they enjoy themselves, giving clear directions and providing variety (change of pace).[7] Developing these sorts of teaching skills might be important to you. In addition to instructional techniques, organization and management techniques might have a high priority. For Sitter's[8] student teachers, this meant:

> *successfully getting a group of learners through a lesson or series of lessons within a limited amount of time. It meant creating a classroom climate conducive to learning; maintaining the environment and restoring the climate constructively when necessary.*[9]

In addition to skills, are there certain habits, traits, or characteristics that you want to acquire or modify? Do you believe, as did some of Sitter's[10] student teachers, that your ability to teach will be hindered by a "lack of patience, low tolerance level, shyness, inadequate feelings, insecurities,"[11] "poor time assessment, lack of creativity, general lack of knowledge in either the scope or sequence of content,"[12] "lack of ambition, hyperactivity, aggressiveness, or lack of commitment"?[13] Obviously, attempts to change such personal propensities are at best frustrating and at worst impossible. But identifying them and explicitly working on them in a field experience might at least allow you to accept them and then to compensate for them.

▶

*Goal 5: To develop your own approach or style*

What makes you unique as a teacher? What do you stand for and believe in?

▶

This goal is actually something that you will achieve as you work through this book. Your own personal perspective on teaching is, in one sense, your own approach. What approaches to, or styles of, teaching would you like to learn about in the process of developing your own? Can you find anyone who epitomizes your ideal teacher?

▶

*Goal 6: To apply what you have learned in college to real learners and to real classrooms*

Are there any specific concepts or theories you want to apply—for example, theories of group dynamics, developmental theories, personality theories, learning theories, motivational theories, or sociological theories? What will you look for in your field experience in order to make the application?

▶

Having considered all these goals, try to specify your personal goals, and list them in order of priority.

▶

For example, consider the following goals mentioned by one prospective elementary school student teacher:

- To learn more about implementing a language-experience approach to reading
- To work on some sort of "discipline technique"—learning to feel out where

you have to draw the line and how far it can go before you have to start saying "all right, sit down," etc.

- To become more sensitive to the feelings and needs of individual children ("getting to know the children faster")
- To develop more confidence as a teacher—specifically, wanting to develop the ability to "change course" in the middle of a lesson when the children do not respond to what has been planned

Keeping your goals in mind, write down your plans to reach these goals, or at least to move in that direction.

▶

## NOTES

1. Andrew Schwebel, Bernice Schwebel, Carol Schwebel, Milton Schwebel, *The Student Teacher Handbook* (New York: Barnes and Noble, 1979), pp. 20-24.
2. Janet Sitter, "The Student Teaching Experience from the Perspective of the Student Teacher: A Descriptive Study." Unpublished doctoral dissertation, Michigan State University, 1982.
3. Ibid.
4. Ibid., p. 127.
5. Ibid.
6. Ibid.
7. Ibid., pp. 136-139.
8. Ibid.
9. Ibid., p. 139.
10. Ibid.
11. Ibid., p. 148.
12. Ibid., p. 149.
13. Ibid.

chapter *3*

# Reflecting on Field Experiences: Fieldwork Logs

Experience + Reflection = Growth

As this equation suggests (and as John Dewey has argued), we do not actually learn from experience as much as we learn from reflecting on experience.

This chapter will help you to document and begin to reflect on your field experience. There are many possible ways to become more reflective about teaching. This book uses two methods, in-text questions/exercises and logs or journals. Before these methods are explained, however, an explanation of reflective thinking is necessary.

## WHAT IS REFLECTIVE THINKING
## AND WHY IS IT DESIRABLE?

Reflective thinking means "turning a subject over in the mind and giving it serious and consecutive consideration."[1] Dewey insists that reflective thinking frees us from mere "impulsive" and "routine activity."[2] "It enables us to act in deliberate and intentional fashion" to achieve what we need. It distinguishes us as human beings and is the hallmark of intelligent (as opposed to mere "appetitive, blind and impulsive") action.[3]

Nonreflective teachers rely on routine behavior and are guided more by impulse, tradition, and authority than by reflection. They simplify their professional lives by uncritically accepting everyday reality in schools. They can then "concentrate their efforts on finding the most effective and efficient means to achieve ends and to solve problems that have largely been defined for them by others."[4] In contrast, reflective teachers actively, persistently, and carefully consider and reconsider beliefs and practices "in light of the grounds that support them and the further consequences to which they lead."[5]

Reflective thinking allows the teacher to examine critically the assumptions that schools make about what can count as acceptable goals and methods, problems, and solutions. Although we all must live within some constraints, often we accept as predetermined by authority or tradition far more than is necessary.

In your field experience, reflective thinking will allow you to act in deliberate and intentional ways, devise new ways of teaching rather than being a slave to tradition, and interpret new experiences from a fresh perspective.

As suggested by the equation that begins this chapter, reflection with no experience is sterile and generally leads to unworkable conclusions. Experience with no reflection is shallow and at best leads to superficial knowledge. If you merely "do" your field experience without thinking deeply about it, if you merely allow your experiences to wash over you without savoring and examining them for their significance, then your growth will be greatly limited. The logs you write, the questions you try to answer, and other activities in which you engage are all merely tools to facilitate reflective thinking about your field experience.

## Is It Possible for an Effective Teacher to Reflect?

As necessary as reflective teaching may seem to some people, others are unconvinced. They argue that there is no *time* for reflection if at the same time you must teach effectively, that there is no *point* for reflection if you always have to do what you are told anyway, and that reflection is not *necessary*, because you can be a good teacher without it. Let us examine these three objections one at a time.[6]

*Is There Time?*   Philip Jackson[7] reminds us that classrooms are busy places:

> [An elementary] teacher engages in as many as 1000 interpersonal interchanges each day. . . . Teaching commonly involves talking and the teacher acts as a gatekeeper who manages the flow of the classroom dialogue. . . . Another time-consuming task for the teacher . . . is that of serving as supply sergeant. Classroom space and material resources are limited and the teacher must allocate these resources judiciously. . . . Broken pens and parched throats obviously do not develop one at a time in an orderly fashion. . . . Closely related to the job of doling out material resources is that of granting special privileges to deserving students. In elementary classrooms it is usually the teacher who assigns coveted duties, such as serving on the safety patrol, or running the movie projector, or clapping the erasers. . . . A fourth responsibility of the teacher is that of serving as an official timekeeper. In many schools he is assisted in this job by elaborate systems of bells and buzzers. But even when the school day is mechanically punctuated by clangs and hums, the teacher is not entirely relieved of his responsibility.[8]

Jackson further points out that this "beehive of activity" is necessitated by the "crowded condition" of the classroom. It is the "press of numbers and of time that keeps the teacher so busy."[9]

As if the realities of classrooms were not enough, institutional constraints further limit the teacher's time for reflection. Teachers are rarely granted released time for reflection. There is continual pressure to cover a specified curriculum and to ensure that a highly diverse group of children—who attend school by compulsion rather than voluntarily—attain at least a minimal level of achievement.

Jackson (among others) argues that, given these conditions, there is no time for reflection and that reflection, if attempted, could only lead to paralysis of action and therefore less effective response to immediate circumstances.[10]

The immediacy of classroom life, the fleeting and sometimes cryptic signs on which the teacher relies for determining his pedagogical moves and for evaluating the effectiveness of his actions calls into question the appropriateness of using conventional models of rationality to depict the teacher's classroom behavior when a teacher is standing before his students. . . . The spontaneity, immediacy and irrationality of the teacher's behavior seems to be its most salient characteristics. At such times there appears to be a high degree of uncertainty, unpredictability, and even confusion about the events in the classroom.[11]

But Jackson is also careful to point out another aspect of teaching:

The fact that the teacher does not appear to be very analytic or deliberative in his moment-to-moment dealings with students should not obscure the fact that there are times when this is not true. During periods of solitude, in particular, before and after his face-to-face encounter with students, the teacher often seems to be engaged in a type of intellectual activity that has many of the formal properties of a problem-solving procedure. At such moments the teacher's work does look highly rational.

This brief mention of the teacher's behavior during moments when he is not actively engaged with students calls attention to an important division in the total set of teaching responsibilities. There is a crucial difference it would seem between what the teacher does when he is alone at his desk and what he does when his room fills up with students.[12]

Research is increasingly confirming the belief that the quality of teacher planning outside the classroom (what Jackson terms the "preactive" phase of teaching) influences the quality of teaching within the classroom (what Jackson terms the "interactive" phase).[13]

Furthermore, despite the time constraints of classroom life, a certain degree of reflection is still possible in the "interactive" phase of teaching. There are always lulls in the action, and even the fast pace of teaching requires some self-evaluation. To consider only the extremes of too much thought and blind action is to limit our options. Clearly, there needs to be a balance between thought and action.

***What's the Point?***   Some people argue that there is little point in reflecting on goals and practices when all the teacher does is implement someone else's ideas. They contend that "teachers are basically functionaries within a bureaucratic system; they have prescribed roles and responsibilities and in order to survive in that system they must always give way to institutional demands."[14] Furthermore, (some claim) teachers inevitably conform to the norms of the school, which "washes out" any reflectiveness left over from preservice training.[15]

Although it is true that schools do socialize new teachers into a dominant "teacher culture," there is a wide range of viewpoints represented in that culture.[16] Teachers within the same school vary widely in evaluation and classroom management practices, goals, political beliefs, treatment of special pupils, adherence to textbooks, and friendliness versus businesslike roles. Surely there is ample room for teachers to exercise individuality in teaching while working within the constraints of schools.

As with our discussion of time, there are two extremes on this issue. According to one view, every teacher is an individual, a person who is free to implement an educational philosophy by teaching what and how he or she wishes. Counter to this sociologically naive view is the position that the forces of bureaucratic socialization in schools are strong and efficient.[17] As with most extreme views, there exists a more moderate position. This view asserts the "constant interplay between choice and constraint" in teaching.[18] Teachers, as professionals working within a powerful institution, have the opportunity to shape their identity, to take a stand even when they are in conflict with others, and to question common practices. Yes, teachers do implement someone else's ideas, but there is always room for personal judgment, decision, and criticism.

Recent psychological research supports this view. In contrast to both a behavioristic view (see B. F. Skinner's *Beyond Freedom and Dignity*) that a person's behavior is totally shaped by the environment, and a humanistic view (see Carl Rogers's *Freedom to Learn in the 1980s*) that a person is free to respond as he or she chooses, a cognitive view stresses the interplay between the individual and the environment. In particular, this view suggests that the individual monitors his or her own actions and thought processes and actively makes decisions about what, and even how, to think.

This latter aspect of mental activity psychologists term *metacognition,*[19] which simply means thinking about thinking. Metacognition in teaching includes the ability of teachers to examine their own concepts, theories, and beliefs about teaching, learning, and their subject matter, and the ability to monitor their decisions about what and how they teach. In a sense, metacognition is a psychological approach to reflective teaching.

***Is It Really Necessary?***   Many claim that reflection is not necessary for teaching. Intuition, they argue, is more important for effective teaching than careful analytic thought. In fact, some of the very best teachers do not seem to spend time reflecting on their work.

Much of this argument, and my response to it, follows the earlier discussion of time available for reflection. But there is more. Anybody who has tried to persuade a group of teachers to implement a particular curriculum has remarked at the degree to which teachers *adapt* rather than *adopt* curricula. Some curriculum developers have even gone to the extreme of attempting (in vain) to produce so-called teacher-proof curricula, an effort I view as an affront to the profession of teaching. That such attempts have been generally unsuccessful seems to be sufficient evidence that teachers are very selective about what they will incorporate into their classrooms. Teachers work within a practicality ethic that subjects any innovation to a test of cost versus benefit, feasibility, and consistency within the teachers' perceptions of themselves and their situations.[20] It is no wonder, then, that most innovations are "blunted on the classroom door."[21] The view of teachers that emerges from studies of curriculum implementation is one of active professionals constantly making educational decisions for their particular classrooms.

Once again, the two extremes are unworkable. Teachers operate neither on pure intuition nor on pure rational analysis. Teachers neither blindly adopt the materials and methods developed by "experts," nor insist on reinventing the wheel. Instead, teachers (especially effective ones) balance intuitive and reflective thought, using any resources they can find and adapting materials to suit their own purposes and methods.

## How Do I Become More Reflective?

As was mentioned earlier, there are two principal means used to help you reflect on your field experience: in-text questions/exercises and logs. You will find questions and exercises designed to encourage reflective thought throughout the text. If you take these questions and exercises seriously, you will find yourself engaged in an inquiry about teaching that ultimately requires a degree of self-analysis and appraisal. The questions and exercises will lead you to develop a sense of approach to your teaching, a "perspective" that will help you define your professional identity. If you pursue a career in teaching and continue to reflect on your professional experience, then your perspective will change over the years. These changes will constitute an important aspect of professional growth.

But, because different situations require different perspectives, there is a danger in making vague generalizations about teaching. You need a way to focus a perspective on specific field experiences rather than on teaching in general. Your daily or weekly logs will help you use your field experience as a specific reference point for your perspective. When you finish this field experience, you probably will not have developed a comprehensive framework for all of education, but most likely you will have determined where you stand and what you believe in with regard to your specific situation. This will be no small accomplishment!

Daily or weekly logs, journals, or some such method for recording events and personal reactions is one widely used method. Although somewhat time consuming, written records and analyses provide a unique opportunity to keep track of events and to privately reflect on the personal and public meaning of those events. What happened? Why did it happen? What was my role? What beliefs did my actions reflect? Did my actions reflect beliefs and assumptions about which I was not aware? Did the consequences of my actions raise doubts or reinforce my beliefs? How should I act in the future on the basis of what happened?

## WHEN SHOULD I WRITE MY LOGS?

Memories are most reliable if you write them down soon after the experience. Therefore, the longer you wait to jot down what happened, the less likely it is that you will remember the details accurately. A full description is not necessary at this point. However, if you intend to include quotations or detailed sequences of events, find a few minutes as soon as possible after the experience to note these details. This is not the time to reflect on the experience. Actually, if you allow some time to pass before you analyze the experience, you may gain insight and write a more thoughtful analysis.

The person who supervises your field experience may have a preferred or required format for your log or journal. Obviously, if this is the case, you should follow it.

However, if you have a relatively free hand in terms of format, the next section suggests one approach.

## WHAT IS THE ANATOMY OF A LOG?

Because a lesson seems unproblematic, even uneventful, it does not mean that there is nothing to observe. The essence of observation is the creation of insight out of what might seem to be routine and commonplace. Hidden beneath the surface of this lesson are unresolved issues, which when they are made visible reveal possible alternative beliefs, values, and practice.[22]

It does not matter if we call it a log or a journal. What does matter is to have an opportunity to think about field experiences. It is difficult to think deeply about all our experiences. Therefore, I suggest a format that helps to focus thoughts on particularly significant events. Focusing on one or two events does not mean ignoring all others. Instead, it means keeping a record of all events while selecting, elaborating, and analyzing one or two that represent an important development in perspective, goals, or plans. Thus, the following format is designed to help you grow as a teacher by enabling you to benefit from your field experiences.

### Fieldwork Log Format

#### A. Heading

Name: (This is unnecessary if you keep your logs in a bound notebook.)

Date of field experiences reported: (A log entry should cover only one day and should be written the day of the experience. Otherwise memories tend to fade.)

Time spent: (e.g., 1:30–3:00 P.M.)

#### B. Sequence of Events

Make a brief list describing what happened. By making a list, you keep a record of what happened. This record may be useful for future reference. It allows you to mention all events, even those that seemed insignificant at the time.

### C. Elaboration of One or Two Significant Episodes

An episode is an "event or sequence of events complete in itself but forming part of a larger one."[23] Select one or two episodes that are significant to you. An episode may be significant because what happened bothers you, excites you, causes you to rethink your initial ideas (i.e., your perspective, goals, or plans), or convinces you that your initial ideas were valid. Therefore, whether the episodes reflect your successes or your failures, they are significant if you learned something important from them.

Once you have selected one or two significant episodes, you should describe them in detail. When you describe the episode, try to relive it. Reliving the experience will enable you to provide as much detail as possible. Make certain that you include what people said, what they did, and how they looked. Try to be as specific as possible, including word-for-word quotations, as best you can remember. Recall what we said earlier about jotting notes as soon as possible. This type of description will provide you with material for reflection in the next section of the log.

Good descriptions should address all four common features (see Chapter 1), or at least you should have considered each. There is a tendency to provide descriptions that are too narrow, focusing only on what the teacher did or said. What we are looking for is a more complete description. Regarding subject matter, if the learner is working on a math problem, include the problem itself in this section. If not, at least describe the content of the "lesson" and the materials with which the learner is working. Regarding the learners, describe what they are saying and doing. Regarding the context, describe the surroundings including any relevant features, such as possible distractions or factors that may contribute to or detract from the teaching atmosphere.

In this description try to avoid inferences about how people felt or what they thought (including your own feelings and thoughts). Save these inferences for the next section, "Analysis."

### D. Analysis of Episode(s)

An analysis of episodes includes an interpretation of what feelings and thoughts may have caused the episodes to occur, why they were significant, what questions they raise, and what you think you learned from them.

Try to figure out what you accomplished, identify problems that emerge and how you plan to follow up, and distill from the episodes what you learned. This last point is the most important. You may have learned what does and does not work in this situation. If so, describe what you conclude. But you may also have learned something about your philosophy of teaching (your perspective). Does the episode confirm your ideas or force you to reconsider them? Maybe some initial ideas you held rather dogmatically depend, to a large extent, on the situation in which you apply them. If so, what was it about the situation that affected the applicability of the ideas? Perhaps the episode relates to something you read or learned about in this or some other education course. This would be the place to discuss it. Many experiences raise more questions than they answer. You might use your logs as an opportunity to note questions arising during your field experiences that you want to discuss with your supervisor or bring up at a field experience seminar.

This suggested format requires you to distinguish between description and analysis, each with its own section of the log. When students begin writing logs, they typically have difficulty distinguishing between these two sections. When they do, they run the risk of undermining the use of their logs for reflection. Some problems include:

1. They add so much analysis to their "Episode" section that they neglect a full description of the episode. Or, they add so much description of episodes to their "analysis" section that they never get a chance to analyze the episode.
2. They make unexamined assumptions in the "Episode" section without giving themselves the opportunity to reflect on those assumptions critically.

## CRITERIA FOR EVALUATING FIELDWORK LOGS

When I read students' logs I use the following criteria in evaluating them:

A. Are all the *parts* there?
   1. Heading
   2. Sequence of events
   3. Episode
   4. Analysis
B. Episode description
   1. Are all *four common features* noted? Learners (what they said and did), Cooperating Teacher (when appropriate), Subject Matter (content of the lesson), Context (surroundings).
   2. Is it *detailed*? Use of quotes, rich description.
   3. Does it *stick to description,* rather than confounding description with analysis. Look especially for instances where the writer attributes (a) a particular motivation (e.g., "trying to please"), (b) a trait (e.g., "lazy"), (c) capabilities (e.g., "a good reader"), or emotional states (e.g., "angry") to the learners.
C. Analysis
   1. Does the analysis *focus on the episode described* earlier (rather than adding additional episode descriptions)?
   2. Does the analysis go beyond simply describing how the writer felt about the experience to include *why* he or she felt that way?
   3. Does the analysis include any *conclusions* from the experience? Conclusions may be in the form of questions that the writer is left with, or dilemmas that the writer realizes, rather than just hard-and-fast principles.
   4. Does the analysis draw on past experiences, readings, or exercises from teacher *education coursework*?

**5.** Does the analysis lead to any *plans?* Will the writer do something as a consequence of this experience the next time he or she teaches?

Keep in mind that these are only guidelines; they should not be considered a formula for writing logs. Every teaching situation is different.

By reading some actual logs written by my students, you may get a clearer idea of how a log looks and what you might include in your own. For this reason sample logs are included in Appendix B.

Toby Fulwiler's Introduction to *The Journal Book* is an especially useful resource on using logs for reflection.[24]

## NOTES

1. John Dewey, *How We Think: A Restatement of the Relation of Reflective Thinking to the Educative Process* (Boston: D. C. Heath, 1933), p. 3.
2. Ibid., p. 17.
3. Ibid.
4. Carl Grant and Kenneth Zeichner, "On Becoming a Reflective Teacher," in *Preparing for Reflective Teaching,* ed. Carl A. Grant (Boston: Allyn and Bacon, 1984), p. 4.
5. Ibid.
6. I am indebted to Grant and Zeichner (ibid.) for the main points of this section.
7. Philip Jackson, *Life in Classrooms* (New York: Holt, Rinehart and Winston, 1968).
8. Ibid., pp. 11-12.
9. Ibid., p. 13.
10. Grant and Zeichner, "On Becoming a Reflective Teacher," p. 9.
11. Jackson, *Life in Classrooms,* pp. 151-152.
12. Ibid., p. 151 (italics in original).
13. Christopher Clark and Penelope Peterson, "Teachers' Thought Processes," in *Handbook of Research on Teaching,* 3rd ed., ed. Merlin Wittrock (New York: Macmillan, 1986), chapter 9.
14. Grant and Zeichner, "On Becoming a Reflective Teacher," p. 10.
15. Ibid.
16. Ibid., p. 11.
17. Wayne Hoy and William Rees, "The Bureaucratic Socialization of Student Teachers," *Journal of Teacher Education* 28 (Jan.-Feb. 1977), pp. 23-26.
18. Ibid., p. 11.
19. John Bransford, *Human Cognition* (Belmont, Calif.: Wadsworth, 1979), pp. 194-203.
20. Walter Doyle and Gerald Ponder, "The Ethic of Practicality: Implications for Curriculum Development," in *Curriculum Theory,* eds. Alex Molnar and John Zahorik (Washington, D.C.: Association for Supervision and Curriculum Development, 1977).
21. John Goodlad and Frances Klein, *Behind the Classroom Door* (Washington, Ohio: Jones Publishing, 1970).
22. Rob Walker and Clem Adelman, *A Guide to Classroom Observation* (London: Methuen, 1975), p. 18.
23. *Webster's New World Dictionary of the American Language,* 2nd college ed. (Englewood Cliffs, N.J.: Prentice-Hall, 1970), p. 471.
24. Toby Fulwiler, ed., *The Journal Book* (Portsmouth, N.H.: Heinemann, 1987).

part **II**

# What Do You Bring to the Experience?

# chapter 4

# Personal Influences on a Perspective

No one's mind is empty. This statement of the obvious applies to both the novice and the expert. We have ideas and ideals about such things as parenting, marriage, coaching, and appropriate bedside manner, even though we may never have been an official parent, spouse, coach, or doctor. The same can be said of teaching. We all have some beliefs about what good teaching is, whether or not we have official status as a "teacher."

Our own beliefs, principles, and ideals (termed "perspective"), however unexamined or incomplete they may now be, function for each of us as a personal "platform." They justify and unify our decisions and actions (just as a political platform does). A personal platform is what we stand for and what we stand on.[1]

A perspective also functions as a lens through which we look at the world of teaching. As a lens, a perspective affects our perception and interpretation of teaching. It does this by forming expectations of what we will experience (the *what* question), by helping us to understand basic reasons for the nature of the experience (the *why* question), and by offering standards for judging the quality of the experience (the *how well* question). Although some distortion is inevitable with any lens, without one we would see only what William James called "bloomin', buzzin' confusion." By becoming aware of the perspective by which we operate, we can at least become sensitive to the bases for our own approach to teaching and, at best, become capable of changing our approach as we gain both new ideas and new teaching experiences. The primary goal of this chapter is to help you begin thinking about your own perspective on teaching; this thinking will make your perspective more explicit and thereby help to clarify it and reconsider its validity.

Where do perspectives come from? To be frank, the answer has me puzzled. Clearly, past experience helps to shape perspectives. This chapter represents an attempt to help you understand the role of your past experiences in forming your present beliefs about teaching. Admittedly, I do not fully understand why some experiences have more impact than others or why different people experience the same set of events differently. But even without understanding the nature of human experience and its relation to perspectives, it is safe to claim that past experience is significant and that thinking about past experiences can contribute to the identification and examination of current perspectives on teaching.

This chapter will be the first step in the initial formulation of your own perspective. There will be no "correct" answers to any of the exercises. Instead, they are intended to guide your thinking about your own approach to teaching, your own beliefs, ideals, commitments, principles, and values. In doing the exercises, you will examine two kinds of teaching-related experiences you have already had. First, you have had extensive experience as a learner. Second, you have had some limited, mostly informal, experience as a teacher.

## EXPERIENCE AS A LEARNER

Those who cannot remember the past not only relive it; they tend to impose it, mistakes and all, on others.[2]

Not all learning is accompanied by teaching. In fact, some of our most potent learning experiences have taken place in the absence of any "teachers" (in both the formal and informal sense). There is no doubt, however, that much learning depends on effective teaching. We can examine our beliefs on learning and teaching by thinking about our own past experience as learners.

---

### EXERCISE 4.1 Significant Learning Experiences

You might try to think about some potent learning experiences you have had. To do this, consider all experiences in which you learned something very significant, something that has stayed with you. A comprehensive list of settings is impossible, but let me try to help jog your memory. Consider the following contexts and people:

1. *Schools*—teachers in and out of classrooms, coaches, or extracurricular activities
2. *At home*—your parents, siblings, grandparents, and other relatives
3. *Chance meetings*—for example, people met while traveling
4. *Religious groups or events*—Sunday school, religious services, talks with religious leaders
5. *Workplaces*—bosses, fellow workers, customers
6. *Libraries*—school projects, pursuing a personal interest, or just plain browsing
7. *Music instruction*—classes, self-instruction, informal teachers
8. *Friendships*—peers, friends much older or much younger than you
9. *Counseling*—e.g., psychological, legal, or drug counselors

Spend 5 or 10 minutes writing down the three most potent and significant learning experiences you can recall. Each experience should have had relatively discrete duration, that is, a time during which you were learning something important to you.

▶

When I have asked my own students to do this exercise, roughly one-third have mentioned one of their college teachers; one-fourth mentioned one of their elementary or secondary school teachers; one-fourth mentioned one of their family members, especially their mothers or fathers; one-fourth mentioned a nonschool music or sports teacher; and one-tenth mentioned a close friend. For many of my students, the significant learning experiences have no teacher. The conditions for a powerful learning experience are apparently set by such factors as the intensity of the situation, the person's own emotional state, and being on one's own. For example, many students mention their first year in college or the death of a friend, relative, or pet as powerful learning experiences.

What follows is the work of three students who were asked to do this exercise. Perhaps reading their work will help you to see what types of experiences qualify and how to describe them.

### *STUDENT RESPONSE 1*

*Taking a course in critical thinking and analytical writing during my first semester in college.* The classroom setting was not crucial to the learning experience, and most of the learning was done by working on essays. The experience was special to me in that I felt I had created something unique, a product of my own thinking that no one could have constructed in the same way. At the time, I was eager to learn this subject and to learn if I could make it in college at all.

*The sudden death of a close friend in my hometown.* I learned how close death can really be and that no loved one should be taken for granted. The setting was crucial to the experience in that I attended the funeral and Mass and saw how others experienced it also. The learning was personal in that the person involved meant a lot to me. I needed to learn why I felt the way I did about his dying, searching for reasons for these feelings.

*The setting was my home when I took up the hobby of silent motion picture collecting and reading.* I absorbed a tremendous amount of information on the subject which, even 13 years later, comes easily to mind. At the time (1969) I was one year shy of draft eligibility and consciously interested in learning about other, better times.

### STUDENT RESPONSE 2

The three most potent learning experiences were *learning sign language, learning how to be a better friend, and learning about my father's World War II experiences.*

I learned sign language in a classroom situation and from working with hearing-impaired students. This learning experience would be considered to be "subject matter." It is also a way of getting to know hearing-impaired people and helping them to get along better. I felt a strong need to learn so that I could communicate with the students on the only level they know how.

Learning how to be a better friend sounds vague and also like something that would take a lifetime. A very special friend gave me a crash course *just* by being my friend. She taught me a lot about myself. She taught me how to be a listener, how to be understanding and giving, and to be less selfish.

Learning about my father's WW II experiences was very important to me because not only did I learn about his life, I learned that he can be very open, given the opportunity. I learned from him while driving from Cornell to my home. I'll always cherish the experience because it was the first time in my life my father actually told me about something very emotional and important to him.

### STUDENT RESPONSE 3

*My first potent learning experience occurred when I was taking piano lessons from a blind man who was teaching me to play songs by ear.* Usually, I would tell him that I wanted to learn a certain song I heard on the radio, and he would play it on the piano while taping what he was playing. I would take the tape home and learn the song. Finally, one day I asked him to teach me a certain song, and he told me to buy the single and learn it myself (without him as an intermediate step). I did this and was successful. I no longer needed his help to take what I was hearing (many different instruments) and play it on the piano. This was important because it set the stage for my future as a musician—playing by ear is sometimes very convenient. It also helped me to write my own music, indirectly.

*Another experience was when I learned the quantum theory of the elements.* I was having a difficult time grasping it and was feeling frustrated and stupid. A teacher of mine kept patiently explaining it to me, and when it finally became clear, I felt like shouting "Eureka!" through the halls of the school.

*A third experience was when I learned to windsurf.* This was important to me because I'm not very athletic, and I felt like I was broadening my horizons. I had a teacher who imparted the basic knowledge, but I learned mostly by practicing with this knowledge in mind (got very wet in the process!). When I finally got the hang of it, I was very proud because others were trying it too—some not as successfully—and I sort of made it look easy!

Next, you might profit from analyzing your three learning experiences. For example, try to identify and write down why each was potent for you. You might warm up for this analysis by first trying it on the three sample responses you have just read. What elements made each experience significant? Consider the following:

- *Context.* In what setting did each experience occur? In a classroom or elsewhere? Was the setting crucial to the experience?

▶

- *Teacher.* Who was involved? Were you alone or with others? Did a "teacher" bring about an experience, did you do it, or did it happen spontaneously?

▶

- *Subject matter.* Was there anything special about what you learned? Did the learning fall under the rubric of "subject matter," or was the learning more unusual and/or personal?

▶

- *Learner.* Was there anything unique about you at the time of each experience? For example, did you feel an especially strong need to learn?

▶

Next, try to draw generalizations about the conditions under which you learn best. Do you find any similarities, or was each experience and learning process unique?

▶

When I have asked undergraduate students to do this exercise, roughly half of the learning experiences have turned out to be instances of either learning without a teacher or learning with a nonschool teacher. Clearly, students bring to our classrooms things they have learned outside classrooms as well as inside other classrooms. We all know this fact, but we all seem to forget it periodically.

On the basis of this exercise, consider your uniqueness as a learner and how this might affect your teaching. How have your past learning experiences affected your views on teaching? For example, as a consequence of your experiences, how important is it for teaching to involve the following:

1. A close relationship with the teacher
2. Being intrinsically motivated to learn

**3.** Learning nonacademic subject matter
**4.** Intense emotion surrounding the learning experience
**5.** A feeling of competence or success by the learner

If your past learning experiences have strongly affected your views, consider the validity of generalizing the conditions under which *you* learn best to conditions of learning for others. In particular, consider the limitations imposed by classroom teaching on providing the conditions required for your most significant learning experiences. Which of your conclusions are generalizable to most public school classroom teaching?

▶

Now we look more specifically at your past classroom teachers, because it is likely that they have contributed a great deal to your conceptions about teaching. It is experiences with past classroom teachers that constitute what Dan Lortie[3] describes as the 13,000-hour "apprenticeship by observation" that people experience before they even reach college.

---

**EXERCISE 4.2   Most Successful and Unsuccessful Teachers**

Try to think back over your 13 to 16 years of elementary, secondary, and higher education. Try to identify the two or three most unsuccessful teachers you can remember. Write their names, or some identifying characteristics if you cannot remember their names. Now jot down next to each what made that person so unforgettable. Do you think most of his or her other students would agree with you, or was your response to this teacher somewhat special? Was this teacher successful with any students? If so, what makes them different from you? What was the subject matter? Was this a factor in your response? Were there special circumstances with regard to community, the school, the class, the teacher's personal life, or your own state of mind? Would you find this teacher just as intolerable today?

▶

Now try to think of the two or three most successful teachers you have ever had. Jot their names down or write something down to identify each of them. What made each of them so successful? What did each of them teach? Was the subject matter a factor in each teacher's success? Do you think other students responded to these teachers as favorably as you? Who might disagree, and how are these students different from you? Were there any special circumstances such as a new and exciting curriculum or special events occurring in the school, community, or world (e.g., space shots, book censorships, a science fair)? Would you find each of these teachers just as wonderful today?

Look over your two lists and notes. What did the teachers do that made them successful or unsuccessful? What can you conclude about teaching?

▶

If you have the opportunity, compare your conclusions with those of your present classmates. Discuss with them what makes your conclusions, and therefore your perspective on teaching, different from theirs. Consider the extent to which your school experiences have contributed to your views about teaching. To what extent have you examined these views? Often we operate from a set of assumptions that affect our expectations, judgments, and preferences of which we are not even aware. It is one thing to operate from a set of unexamined beliefs and another to hold on to those beliefs dogmatically in the face of contrary evidence. As long as we remain tentative about our beliefs and continually try to test them, we continue to grow.

Many of the beliefs we hold as teachers are derived from our experiences as students. In Appendix A you will respond to a set of statements designed to help you identify your perspective on your field experience as a teacher (the Teacher Belief Inventory [TBI]). For now we will focus on your perspective on being a student. In Appendix A you will also find the Student Belief Inventory (SBI). Take the time to complete it now.

## FAVORITE SUBJECT MATTER AND TOPICS

It seemed impertinent when on my first day of teaching a student asked, "Why should anyone learn this stuff?" I had no answer, so I told the student to be quiet; he was, and the questioned remained unanswered. However, as the days wore on, the question nagged at me. It was, after all, a good question, no matter what the student's motive was for asking it. We should know why we are taking people's time and consuming the community's resources for teaching particular topics in language arts, social studies, math, science, physical education, vocational education, foreign languages, computer science, home economics, industrial arts, and all the other subjects. At the very least, we ought to know why anyone should learn the particular subject matter and topics we teach.

What are your favorite subject matters? Are you most interested in fiction, poetry, biology, history, mathematics, sports, health, or some other subject matter?

▶

What specific topics interest you the most? F. Scott Fitzgerald's novels, the Civil War, ecology, baseball, space travel, or some other topics?

▶

**EXERCISE 4.3   Most and Least Important Courses Taken**

Think back over your schooling career. Try to identify the five courses or subjects you studied that in retrospect seem most important. Do the same for those you consider least important. *Webster's New World Dictionary* defines *important* as "meaning a great deal; having much significance, consequence or value." The less important, the more trivial, time wasting, and fruitless.

**FORM 4.3**   Most and least important courses

| Most Important | Least Important |
| --- | --- |
| 1. | |
| 2. | |
| 3. | |
| 4. | |
| 5. | |

When I try this exercise with large heterogeneous classes of undergraduates, I receive two lists that are almost identical. That is, every subject that someone considers most important someone else considers least important. My conclusion is that no subject will get universal support. A lot depends on the particular learner.

For each course you listed, examine your reasons for putting it in a particular column.

What criteria for selecting subject matter do your choices imply? Consider the following possibilities:[4]

1. *Context.* Are your choices based on their contribution to further learning (formal or nonformal), to your vocation, or personal-social living? That is, are your choices based on *what* they are useful for?
2. *Further learning.* For those choices related to further learning, are any important because they provide "basic tools" for further learning, or because they offer fundamental ideas (i.e., key concepts or broadly applicable explanations)?
3. *Vocation.* For those choices related to your vocation (or avocation), are any important because they contributed to selection, performance, or upgrading of your vocation/avocation?
4. *Personal-social living.* Are any of your choices based on their contribution to the society or community as a whole while others are based on their contribution to you as an individual? That is, are your choices based on *who* (i.e., society or individual) is supposed to benefit from them?

5. *Use situations.* Are any of your choices based on the frequency or diversity of situations in which you put them to use or how crucial (though possibly rare or unique) the situation is when they are put to use? That is, are your choices based on their *situational usefulness?*
6. *Timing.* Are any of your choices important or unimportant because they are useful at the present time, in the foreseeable future, or in the remote future? That is, are your choices based on *when* they are useful?
7. *Use mode.* Do your choices reflect an emphasis on using knowledge to solve the types of problems and perform the kinds of skills similar to those taught (e.g., vocational training, reading), to provide ideas that enable you to interpret the social and natural world in which you live (e.g., physics), or to provide imagery and other associations that enrich experience (e.g., poetry)?

If these questions help you uncover some of the implicit reasons you value certain subject matter and topics over others, try jotting down these insights here.

▶

Many of these assumptions about education might underlie your justification for teaching particular topics. However, personal history plays a role also.

---

**EXERCISE 4.4    The Road to My Favorite Subject Matter and Topics**

Think back over your life, both in and out of school. Jot down significant events (e.g., a trip to Europe) or people (e.g., a brother-in-law who is a scientist) that have influenced the value you place on your favorite subject matter and topics. That is, what events and people led to your special interests?

**FORM 4.4    Key events and people**

| Events | People |
|--------|--------|
|        |        |

## EXPERIENCE AS A TEACHER

In Chapter 1 you made an inventory of your prior teaching experiences. Now you can examine them as sources of your initial perspective on teaching.

---

**EXERCISE 4.5   Analysis of Prior Teaching Experiences**

For each of the prior teaching experiences you listed in the exercise in Chapter 1, try to analyze the extent and the nature of your success. Remember, we are referring to nonformal teaching in addition to formal teaching. The following form may help you perform this analysis.

**FORM 4.5**   Analysis of prior teaching experiences

| Description of experience (from Form in Chapter 1) | Success rating (1 = Failure) (5 = Success) | Criteria for judging success | Factors in success or failure |
|---|---|---|---|
| 1. | | | |
| 2. | | | |
| 3. | | | |
| etc. | | | |

---

If you performed this analysis, what can you conclude about teaching? On what sorts of success criteria do you typically rely? To what extent do these criteria reflect your views about what is important in teaching? To what extent do these criteria depend on the teaching situations? Are you likely to use these criteria in your field experience?
▶

How successful have you been at teaching? To what extent has your success motivated you to pursue a career in teaching?
▶

What factors have contributed to your successes or failures? How likely is it that these factors will affect your success or failure during your field experience?
▶

To what extent and in what ways have your prior teaching experiences affected your beliefs about and ideals for teaching?

▶

---

### EXERCISE 4.6    The Role of the Media on Beliefs

In addition to the highly personal influences on your beliefs about teaching that we have probed in this chapter, there are also other influences. The next two chapters explore some of these. However, in preparation for these two chapters, consider the role of the media on your beliefs. Think back now about books and magazine articles you may have read and TV programs and movies you may have viewed. Jot down (in the space provided or on a separate sheet of paper) titles, authors, or subjects of pieces of work, as best you can remember them, that have had an impact on your thinking about teaching.

|  | WHAT I REMEMBER ABOUT IT | IMPACT ON MY THINKING |
|---|---|---|
| Books |  |  |
| Articles |  |  |
| TV programs |  |  |
| Movies |  |  |

---

## NOTES

1. Decker Walker, "A Naturalistic Model of Curriculum Development," in *Curriculum: An Introduction to the Field,* ed. James Gress (Berkeley, Calif.: McCutchan, 1978).
2. Eliot Wigginton, *The Foxfire Book* (Garden City, N.Y.: Anchor Books, 1972), p. 10.
3. Dan Lortie, *Schoolteacher* (Chicago: University of Chicago Press, 1975).
4. Mauritz Johnson, *Intentionality in Education* (Albany, N.Y.: Center for Curriculum Research and Services, 1977), pp. 134–135.

# chapter 5

# Contributions
# of Foundational Studies

**M**any teacher-educators believe that a person's perspective on teaching is formed by more than the experiences that the person has had as learner and teacher. They cite the importance of concepts and theories drawn from certain disciplines. After all, they claim, teaching implies helping a student learn things, which, in turn, contributes to the achievement of broader educational aims. Appropriate aims are, at least in part, a *philosophical* issue, and the nature of learning is a *psychological* issue. In addition, teachers and students operate in one of our society's most significant institutions and therefore teachers must take into account the *sociology* of teaching. Awareness of these aspects of teaching leads teacher educators to consider philosophy, psychology, and sociology as three of the "foundations" of teaching. Other foundational studies include the history, economics, and politics of teaching.[1] Most preservice teacher education programs, therefore, require some coursework in at least two or three of these disciplines.

For foundational studies to be useful to field experiences, we must find ways of using foundational studies to help us think about and thereby enrich these experiences. One way that the foundations can do this is by supplying concepts for interpreting a particular field experience. For example, philosophy offers concepts like the scientific method, autonomy, and structure of knowledge; psychology offers concepts such as feedback, transfer, and intrinsic motivation; and sociology offers concepts such as role, bureaucracy, socialization, socioeconomic status, and subculture. If these concepts help us to understand what is going on in a school or in a classroom, then they may be considered useful for the analysis.

Another way to understand the contributions of the foundations is to view them as a source of questions and issues that must be addressed by any thoughtful teacher. For instance, philosophy, among other things, raises questions about the purposes to which teachers should give highest priority—transmission of our cultural heritage, citizenship, self-fulfillment, or vocational development; psychology, among other things, raises questions regarding the effectiveness of competition for improving motivation; and sociology raises questions about such things as the kinds of values, norms, and social definitions implicitly taught through the rules, procedures, and grading practices established by the school and the teacher.

The purpose of this chapter is to help you use your foundational studies as bases for reflection about your field experiences. Although your perspective on teaching could embody a wide range of possible issues, the six issues we discuss encompass many (but not all) dimensions of most teachers' perspectives. We will examine each issue as a possible dimension of your perspective on teaching and in order to identify concepts you might find useful for thinking about it. We will also analyze some possible positions on the issue in order to help you clarify your own position.

The issues we will examine are control, knowledge, learning and motivation, the teacher's role, pupil diversity, and the relation between school and society. These same six issues are used to organize the teacher interview questions in Chapter 11 and the belief inventories in Appendix A.

These six issues can be expressed as questions that a teacher's perspective might address.

## SIX BASIC ISSUES OF TEACHING

1. *Control.* Who should control what goes on in teaching, and what should be the range of their control?
2. *Diversity.* How unique are learners and how should one treat learners on the basis of their differences?
3. *Learning.* How do people learn in terms of both the process of learning and the motivation for it?
4. *Role.* How formal (versus personal) should teachers be in their relationships with the learners?
5. *School and Society.* To what extent do the sources of and solutions to teachers' problems require structural changes in schools or society?
6. *Knowledge.* What is knowledge? Is knowledge a given set of facts, concepts, and generalizations to be transmitted, or is it more a personal or social construction developed by processes of reasoning and negotiation?

Taken as a whole, the six basic issues cover a broad range.[2] We can see this scope by locating each issue on our earlier map of four common features (see Figure 1.1). The issues of student diversity and how students learn clearly center on the *learners.* The teacher's role is obviously an issue centering on the *teacher* and how he or she relates to the learners. School and society issues can be considered primarily *contextual* issues in teaching. Issues regarding the nature of knowledge reflect a dominant concern for conceptions of the *subject matter* we teach. Issues of control cover all four common features.

## Control

- "A teacher who cannot control the class cannot teach."
- "The most important lesson to be learned is respect for authority."
- "In a democratic society, the teacher should make all decisions democratically."

Maybe one or more of these common sayings reflect your own viewpoint on control. When we talk about control in teaching, we are concerned with issues of *who* controls *whom* and in *what areas* they should exert their control. The "who" and "whom" refer to teachers, students, parents, administrators, textbook publishers, and state education personnel, among others. "What areas" refers to the particular domains in which the teachers, students, and others might exert control. Issues of control include the following:

1. Whether or not the teacher is merely an intermediary between the administration or textbook writers and the learner
2. How strict the teacher should be
3. How extensive the teacher's control is (as compared with that of the students, parents, administrators, etc.) in determining the amount of *time* spent on activities and the *rules* of conduct in the classroom (both the number and the kind of rules)
4. Who should select and design classroom activities, the standards used to evaluate performance, and the goals of instruction
5. How closely teachers must adhere to the school's goals and policies

Let us see what light we can expect foundation courses to shed on such questions of control. In an attempt to answer these questions, we will examine sociologically the teacher's rules and the socialization process as a means of controlling students and the curriculum as a means of controlling both teachers and students.

First let us take a quick look at schools through the eyes of a sociologist. To most sociologists the school and the classroom are social systems embedded within broader social systems, that is, the community, state, and nation. Within any social system there is bound to be conflict and, therefore, coercion.[3]

One conflict "exists between the bureaucratic authority of administrators, based on their position in a hierarchy of offices, and the professional authority of teachers, based on their training in a body of theory related to learning."[4] Another conflict derives from the compulsory nature of schooling, "which captures students for a prolonged period." This coercive situation drives students to "form their own subcultures, as a means of coping with the pervasive and systematic demands of school authorities." These subcultures increase the level of conflict, because they typically do not support the educational goals of the school's faculty and staff.

But some sociologists, rather than emphasizing conflict, point out that any social system to some extent depends on a "consensus" of values and beliefs, if that social system is to function.[5] The school attempts to achieve consensus by socializing students, that is, by teaching self-control, discipline, and respect for authority. Of all the beliefs and values the schools try to instill, some consensus theorists consider the most significant to be the belief that achievement is the basis for the allocation of people to occupational slots in the society.[6] However, other, more critical sociologists claim schools reward students not only on the basis of their achievement but also on the basis of their social class.[7] Diverse sociological ideas, stemming from these different sociological theories, provide different bases for thinking about questions of control.

***Rules.***   For the sociologist, rules express norms of behavior. The methods of their enforcement are an expression of the sanctions the teacher chooses to employ. The enforcement of rules, then, is one means by which the teacher deals with the inevitable conflict arising within an autocratic form of governance.[8] Furthermore, the rules teachers enforce reflect the type of socialization process that the school promotes.[9]
Consider the following questions about rules:

What rules do you plan to make explicit to your class?

Should rules be made cooperatively with the class or should they be made only by the teacher?

Do you think you will expect students to follow any rules that you do not plan to state explicitly?

What will be the scope of both your explicit and implicit rules? That is, what will they cover?

Consider the following areas:

- Speaking order
- Movement within the classroom
- Movement outside the classroom
- Arrival time
- Seating posture
- Noise level
- Format and neatness of written work
- Dress
- Manners (student–teacher and student–student)

What sorts of sanctions do you think you might impose on students who break rules? What sorts of sanctions would you never impose?

▶

***Socialization and the Hidden Curriculum.***   Rules are explicit expressions of norms of behavior, but they are also the least effective form of regulation. Sociologists point out that schools prefer to have students follow norms of behavior without coercion. To the extent that the students internalize the school's norms, the need for rules decreases. Students who control themselves require few rules. In a sense, explicit rules cover only those areas for which socialization has been incomplete or ineffective.

You might want to consider the sorts of assumptions you make concerning socialization. For example, consider the sorts of norms you will expect students to follow in the absence of explicit rules.

▶

Often we base our expectations about student behavior on our own past experience. These expectations can lead to many surprises, however, if we happen to teach in a school with a student population much different from the schools we attended. Because the home is the basis for most of the socialization process, the more you know about the community, the better prepared you will be in dealing with your students. (See Chapter 8 for some suggestions on how to learn about the community.)

Some educational sociologists consider the school's norms of behavior to be manifestations of what they call a "hidden curriculum."[10] They claim that the hidden curriculum is a powerful means of "social control." Included within the concept of a hidden curriculum are many outcomes that may result (and may even be expected to result) from the enforcement of both explicit and implicit rules. These potential outcomes may include docility; how to sit still for long periods under crowded conditions; a belief that effort, neatness, and promptness are more important than achievement; a belief that students get what they deserve in school; a belief that one's personality must be kept under constant control; a respect for authority; and many others. You will likely find some of these outcomes desirable, some undesirable, and some controversial. Actually, it depends on your own view of schools. Some people discover the hidden curriculum and exclaim, "Oh, my goodness!", whereas others proclaim, "Thank goodness!"

You might consider the kind of hidden curriculum you would like to discover in schools, the kind you suspect exists but hope does not exist, and what to do with a hidden curriculum when you find one.[11] Your preferred hidden curriculum is an expression of your preferred kinds of social control.

A closely related issue raised by sociologists concerns the hidden curricula of different socioeconomic status (SES) groups. Not only may low-SES groups sometimes receive different official curricula, they may also receive different hidden curricula. Some sociologists examine the rules enforced by teachers in schools within different communities.[12] For example, they find that, in contrast to classrooms in high-SES communities, classrooms in low-SES communities restrict movement more within the class and outside the classroom (e.g., require bathroom passes), allow for less student decision making with regard to topics, allow less independent project work, require more busy work, and allow less student-to-student talk in the classroom.

Consider the ways in which the hidden curricula of low-SES classrooms might differ from that of high-SES classrooms. Contrast what low-SES students might learn with what high-SES students might learn as a consequence of the classroom norms. Would you as a teacher treat low-SES students differently from high-SES students? If not, what do you think accounts for the findings of sociologists? Maybe you are different from the teachers in the sociological studies just mentioned.

▶

***The Curriculum as a Means of Control.***    Norms may be the most obvious means of control, but plans also control. One type of plan is the curriculum. Whether a curriculum is conceived as a plan describing intended instructional methods (i.e., means), intended learning outcomes (i.e., ends), or both, it controls both the teacher and the student by legitimizing some types of content and activities and delegitimizing others.

The more bureaucratically organized the school, the further up the hierarchy important decisions are made. Yet the more teachers seek to professionalize their occupation, the more *they* want to make important decisions themselves. This conflict between teachers and administrators often centers on selection of textbooks, methods, and curriculum. Attempts to "standardize" the curriculum can be seen as attempts to further bureaucratize the school and, thus, to deprofessionalize teachers.

To what extent do you intend to follow the school's curriculum if you happen to disagree with it? To what extent do you believe you should "adjust your teaching to the administration's view of good teaching practice" and be "obedient, respectful, and loyal to the principal" regarding matters of curriculum?[13]

▶

The school's curriculum defines what is to count as "school knowledge," as opposed to "non-school everyday knowledge."[14] For sociologists like Weber,[15] curricula are defined in terms of a dominant group's idea of the "educated person."

Some sociologists are concerned with how the imposition of certain knowledge (i.e., curricula) on lower SES groups prevents these groups from thinking for themselves.[16] These sociologists suggest that the dominant group's "common sense" becomes legitimized by being labeled "school knowledge" (and by being made available to certain groups through the official curriculum), whereas other groups' common sense is ignored.

This sociological perspective goes a step further to describe the sort of knowledge characterized as school knowledge and thereby is included in the school's curriculum. According to these sociologists, knowledge that serves "to legitimate a rigid hierarchy between teacher and taught"[17] is accorded the highest status. Such high-status knowledge is likely to manifest "a clear distinction between what is taken to count as knowledge, and what is not."[18] Furthermore, high-status knowledge is likely (1) to emphasize written rather than oral presentation, (2) to emphasize individual rather than group work in both instruction and evaluation, (3) to be abstract, and (4) to be "at odds with daily life and common experience."[19]

You might consider how you would characterize the subject matter you intend to teach according to this perspective:

1. Its status
2. The students to whom it will and will not be made available
3. The likelihood that different curricula in this subject matter will be offered to different students (e.g., different "tracks")

***Philosophical and Psychological Perspectives on Control.***   This analysis of control-related issues is certainly not exhaustive. For example, the sociological discussion of the teacher's enforcement of rules could have included psychologically based techniques for "managing" classrooms, such as behavior-modification techniques. The predominantly sociological discussion of the teacher's responsibilities for the official curriculum of the state or school could have included philosophical analyses of liberty and academic freedom, including an analysis of who is entitled to control what and for whom.[20] The sociological discussion of knowledge could have included a philosophical analysis of the educated person. It could also have included a psychological analysis of the likely transfer-of-learning (i.e., "generativeness") that different subjects offer or a theoretical account of the relation among knowledge, attitudes, and actions. These discussions only suggest the range of possible contributions to issues of control offered by philosophy, sociology, and psychology.

## Learning and Motivation[21]

If you have ever taken an educational psychology course, then there is likely to be no doubt in your mind that questions regarding learning and motivation are based on psychological theory. Whether they discuss learning or motivation, educational psychology courses often contrast behaviorist and cognitive theories. Behaviorist accounts of learning provide concepts such as the following to describe learning and teaching:

- *Law of exercise:* Repetition of a conditioned response strengthens the bond between the stimulus situation and the response; i.e., practice makes perfect
- *Reinforcement:* Anything that increases the strength of a behavior, with positive reinforcement using rewards and negative reinforcement using the withdrawal of unpleasant situations
- *Partial reinforcement:* Less than 100 percent reinforcement of responses
- *Operant conditioning:* Eliciting behaviors and then reinforcing them
- *Shaping:* Reinforcement of successive steps or approximations toward an ultimate target behavior
- *Modeling:* Providing a demonstration of a behavior for learners to observe and then to imitate
- *Self-pacing:* Pacing placed under learner control
- *Frame:* In programmed learning materials, a step that ends by having learners make an active response
- *Active responses:* A response requiring action (e.g., underlining the correct answer)

These concepts allow us to think about questions regarding teaching. For example, should we rely only on positive reinforcement? How small should our instructional steps be? How much modeling should we use in addition to verbal explanations?

Cognitive theories of learning introduce a different set of concepts. For example:

- *Insight:* Seeing all at once the solution to a problem (i.e., "Aha!")
- *Assimilation:* The incorporation of new ideas into an existing cognitive structure
- *Cognitive structure:* An interrelated set of concepts, beliefs, and information that a person has in his or her mind
- *Cognitive dissonance:* Discrepancy, incongruity, or gap between existing knowledge and a new learning task or experience
- *Spiral curriculum:* Successively returning to an idea at increasing levels of sophistication
- *Reception versus discovery learning:* Presentation of content to learners in final form versus allowing the learners to figure it out for themselves
- *Meaningful versus rote learning:* Content being related to the learner's cognitive structure in a nonarbitrary fashion versus the learner's acquiring information that he or she does not integrate into cognitive structure
- *Advance organizers:* Introductory material that acts as a cognitive framework for subsequent instruction
- *Short- versus long-term memory:* One aspect of information storage that is very limited in capacity versus another aspect of information storage that is virtually unlimited in capacity but from which retrieval is often difficult

These concepts allow us to raise further questions about learning: For example, how can we deepen the learners' insights into the meaning of the content we teach? What sorts of advance organizers will help people learn the new material meaningfully? How much cognitive dissonance is productive?

To make matters more complicated, behaviorists and cognitive learning theorists share certain terminology also, although they typically attach different meanings to each term and reach different conclusions. For example, behaviorists claim that errors should be minimized so as to avoid learning them, whereas cognitivists claim that people learn best from their errors.

Behaviorists and cognitive learning theorists also agree on certain general principles, although they may explain them differently. Thus, they are both likely to claim that attention, modeling, and practice with feedback are likely to improve performance, but they will explain why in very different theoretical terms.

These basic differences would likely result in different views regarding some common teaching practices. For example:

1. *Setting up a laboratory experiment.* Behavioristic approach: The laboratory is for training learners in laboratory skills and scientific behaviors. Cognitive approach: The laboratory gives the learners an opportunity to make a dis-

covery and to confront some evidence that challenges or conflicts with their existing ideas.

2. *Designing or selecting instructional material* (e.g., workbooks, texts, films). Behavioristic approach: Instructional material should build complex skills out of simpler prerequisite skills, attempting to minimize learner errors by proceeding in small enough steps. Cognitive approach: Instructional material should present the entire framework at the outset (perhaps by using an analogy or a good example), with the remainder of the material successively adding refinement, sophistication, and detail to the framework while allowing the students to learn from mistakes and to figure out some things for themselves through intelligent guessing.

3. *Giving tests.* Behavioristic approach: Tests directly measure the attainment of the teacher's objectives, letting the teacher know whether the class has mastered the objective and giving the learner positive reinforcement, thereby increasing the strength of the behavior. Cognitive approach: Tests offer highly indirect indicators of what is really going on inside a learner's head (e.g., conceptual development), allowing the teacher to analyze student misconceptions and errors, and giving the learners information they can use as a basis for modifying ideas and performance. The behaviorist believes that anything with meaning can be observed and measured, whereas the cognitivist believes that many important things we learn are unobservable and therefore cannot be measured in any direct sense.

Consider the following case:

Adrienne's field experience consists of tutoring a ninth-grade boy who is having difficulty with mathematics. Although his class is now studying algebra, the cooperating teacher informs her that Jeff has some gaps in his math preparation. For one thing, he does not seem to know what to do when given a problem requiring the conversion of decimals to fractions and vice versa. Adrienne has found two sets of instructional materials that she can use as a resource for her tutoring session.

One set[22] presents math in programmed form with exercises involving practice drill. Questions are presented in a form that can be answered briefly. For example,

1. Fill in the blanks:
   $3.111 = 3 + 1/10 + 1/100 + 1/1000$ (The first example is a model answer.)
   $7.652 = 7 + 6/\ \ + 5/\ \ + 2/$
   $95.015 = 95 + 0/\ \ + 1/\ \ + 5/$

The second set of materials presents math using drawings and manipulatives in which the learner is expected to make educated guesses, to explain how he or she arrived at a particular answer, and to relate the math content to everyday experiences.

Which materials should Adrienne use with Jeff? What reasons can you give to support your claim? Do you find your preferred approach to this situation to be more behavioristic (the first set of materials) or cognitive (the second set)?

▶

What else do you need to know in order to answer this question? Do you think that your psychological theory depends on the subject matter? What if the subject matter were spelling? What if it were writing?

▶

As expected, behaviorist and cognitive theorists also differ in their explanations of motivation.

> Behavioral psychologists suggest that behavior is determined by past reinforcements and the contingencies in the present environment (i.e., a concern with incentives, habits), . . . and thus more concerned with observable behavior. Cognitive psychologists believe that people decide what they want to achieve, and that their thought processes control behavior. . . [Therefore, they] are most concerned with perceptions (e.g., discrepancies), information processing, understanding, and curiosity.[23]

Thus, whereas behavioral psychologists talk about *selecting* and *fixing responses* through *reinforcement* and *eliminating* or *extinguishing* others,[24] cognitive psychologists talk about how people perceive and think about themselves and about their success.

> Behaviorists place more emphasis upon external rewards and the deliberate and systematic arrangement of reinforcement contingencies, whereas cognitive theorists place more emphasis upon internal rewards and related cognitive processes.[25]

Behaviorists emphasize extrinsic motivation, and cognitivists stress intrinsic motivation. Many cognitivists believe that curiosity is a natural and spontaneous characteristic of all people, especially children. Other, more eclectic educators believe that curiosity and intrinsic interest are unreliable sources of motivation for the majority of learners and extrinsic rewards must be used initially to involve learners in productive tasks. Once involved, the tasks themselves will often supply intrinsic motivation. What is your view?

▶

Whether your view emphasizes extrinsic or intrinsic rewards, you probably have fairly strong beliefs about competition as a motivator. Perhaps you agree with Johnson and Johnson:

> Competition is threatening and discouraging to those who believe they cannot win and many students will withdraw or only half-try in competitive situations. The whole area of intrinsic motivation shows that motivation does not depend upon competition. Even in extrinsic motivation situations, competition will exist only when there is a limited amount of the reinforcer which cannot be shared with everyone, and when everyone believes he has a chance of winning.[26]

If you agree with Johnson and Johnson, you will likely prefer cooperative classroom environments, not only for motivational purposes but also for the contribution of cooperative environments to social development.

However, you may disagree with them and believe instead that competition is a fact of life and that, whether or not it heightens motivation, it is nevertheless an important lesson to be learned in schools in its own right.

Consider your own view of the role of competition and cooperation in the classroom. Think about your own classroom and whether it would emphasize a cooperative or competitive environment. Maybe your answer would vary with different learners.

Consider, for example, some common teaching practices from the perspective of your beliefs about motivation.

1. If you were marking student papers, consider whether you would let the entire class know who did the best or whether individual success should be a private matter. Think about the emphasis of your comments on the papers, whether for reinforcement (e.g., praise), for challenging student responses and for raising further questions, or for both purposes.

▶

2. If you were organizing the classroom for a set of tasks (e.g., experiments, math problems, art projects, map work, etc.), consider whether you would want to organize students into groups or if you would prefer to have them work individually. Would you want students to cooperate on the work or to compete with one another? When choosing the problems or projects on which they work, how important would it be to you that students be initially interested in the work?

▶

Maybe a course in educational psychology has already challenged your beliefs on learning and motivation by presenting alternative views. Maybe such a challenge lies in front of you. Educational psychology has the potential to help you understand the psychological assumptions on which many of your beliefs rest, to help you reconsider those assumptions, and to give you a technical vocabulary to discuss issues of learning and motivation.

## Diversity of Learners

**TEACHER 1:** It's only fair to treat all learners equally.

**TEACHER 2:** Yes, but we must respond to their individual needs.

**STUDENT TEACHER:** But which one of you is right?

In a one-on-one teaching situation, we typically respond to the learner as an individual. When we are faced with 30 learners, the complexity of the situation multiplies geometrically. How we view learners and how we treat them in group situations is crucial to our teaching. Whether we perceive each learner as unique or as a member of a category (e.g., slow, handicapped, poor, disruptive), and whether we treat learners equally regardless of their differences (or differently because of their differences), determines many of our teaching practices. For example, opinions differ about the teacher's allocation of time, based on special learner needs, and the individualization of objectives, content, pace, method of instruction, standards, and rules.

People disagree about special considerations for special learners partly because they disagree about what qualifies as a special need. Both sociology and psychology provide concepts to describe differences among learners; that is, these disciplines provide a variety of labels for categories of "specialness." Although particular schools and agencies have particular policies with regard to special needs, ultimately the teacher decides which of the characteristics are relevant to teaching practices (e.g., what to expect of learners, how much time to give them, and what rules they must follow).

Let us begin with a list of general learner characteristics drawn from psychology and sociology: IQ, gender, socioeconomic status, ethnicity, race, personality type, developmental stage, family lifestyle, attention span, and reading level.

Also consider a list of labels for students drawn from these two disciplines:

gifted and talented
disadvantaged or culturally deprived
learning disabled
anxious
highly verbal
only child
hyperactive
aggressive
concrete operational
creative
dogmatic

Also think about another list, not necessarily drawn from psychology and sociology, but nevertheless part of the everyday language of educators:

"jock"

hardworking or lazy

over- or underachiever

college bound or terminal

bright or slow

immature or serious

Of course, none of these lists is exhaustive. But it is important to remember that there are many possible ways to label and categorize learners.

Some sociologists, by studying particular schools and communities in depth, identify the different ways in which teachers and administrators treat different students, particularly those of differing socioeconomic statuses. These researchers note that, depending on how they categorize a student, teachers apply different rules, employ different sanctions when rules are broken, have different academic and occupational expectations, apply different academic standards, seek different amounts of student input in instructional decision making, allocate different amounts of instructional time, and teach different content. Such practices may tend to limit students' opportunities for upward social mobility and might act as a set of self-fulfilling prophecies regarding the relationship between SES or race and achievement. That is, students may live up to their teachers' expectations.

However, the point is not to claim that we should ignore all differences among learners, avoid individualization, and not tailor our teaching to the learners' needs. Treating learners as unique individuals is not the same as labeling and then treating them as members of groups. By categorizing learners, we might stereotype and obscure their individualities. More important, to some sociologists, labeling and grouping learners runs the risk of limiting the educational opportunity of some students while maximizing it for others. That is, there is always the danger that, despite our good intentions, we may be practicing a subtle form of discrimination.

Do you have different expectations for different groups of students by virtue of their membership in those groups? Do you plan to group learners in your classroom? If so, on what basis? Would the different groups get different amounts of your time or different materials? What undesirable short- or long-term consequences of this differential treatment should you be careful about?

▶

Whether or not you plan to group learners, your class is likely to be a heterogeneous mixture of learners. If you teach more than one class, the classes will differ in composition. How do you plan to deal with the diversity of learners? What is your attitude toward learners from backgrounds different from your own? How could you use their diversity as a resource for your teaching? How could you make your lessons more multicultural?

## Knowledge

The subject matter is typically taken for granted as the stable "stuff" of teaching, and yet it is the center of a very important set of issues affecting daily teaching practice. Traditionally, debates about knowledge in philosophy of education have concerned the nature of truth. Different philosophies propose different views of truth: truth as the coherence of ideas for idealists, truth as correspondence to reality for realists, truth as the product of reason and intuition of neo-Thomists, truth as what works for experimentalists, or truth as existential choice for existentialists.[27]

How do you view knowledge in your subject matter? Do you think of learning your subject matter as absorbing ideas (idealism), mastering facts and information (realism), training the intellect (neo-Thomism), problem solving (experimentalism), or finding the self (existentialism)?[28]

More recently, philosophical debates about knowledge have concerned the way in which scientific ideas change and science progresses. Today's philosophers of science, such as Thomas Kuhn and Stephen Toulmin, reject the nineteenth-century "empiricist" view that science changes as a result of the accumulation of new facts and observations and the refinement of generalizations based on them. They also reject the empiricist requirement that scientists observe what is "really there" and be objective in their descriptions. In contrast, modern philosophy of science contends that science changes as a result of the failure of current theory to solve important scientific problems. Old theories are rejected and replaced by new ones based on assumptions significantly different from those of the theories they are replacing. This "conceptual change" view argues further that our concepts and theories determine what we see. People with different theories can live in different perceptual worlds. Thus, what scientists see is affected by their scientific theories and concepts.[29]

These philosophical views have important implications for teaching practice. Consider, for example, three contrasting views on teaching as they relate to empiricist and conceptual change philosophies of science.[30]

A *didactic* view of teaching, primarily aimed at transmitting knowledge, relies on clear explanations, experiments, or demonstrations employed in support of the explanations, and guides discussions by using convergent questions, hints, and explanations. This view assumes learning to be the addition of new knowledge—a view consistent with empiricist ideas about the growth of knowledge.

A *discovery* view of teaching assumes that "students develop knowledge for themselves through active investigation and discovery."[31] The teacher focuses on student observations and measurements, acceptance of student responses to questions, and an absence of teacher presentations. This view is also fundamentally empiricist, particularly in its emphasis on objective observations "uncontaminated" by theories and in its claim that knowledge develops inductively from observations.

Both of these views have been criticized by the *interactionist* view,[32] a view based on a conceptual change philosophy. The *interactionist* view of teaching argues that students arrive in the classroom with well-formed, though often incorrect, ideas. Didactic teaching rejects or ignores these ideas. Discovery teaching allows students to develop further and refine their naive ideas through active experimentation, whether or not their naive ideas are true. In contrast with these two views, the *interactionist* view is more adversarial, recognizing the necessary interaction among students' naive ideas, their empirical observation, and the curriculum content. Such a view requires the teacher

> to bring out the students' preconceptions, provide a base of relevant experience and observations, challenge the students' misconceptions with appropriate questions and evidence, clearly present the . . . conception (to be learned), and help the student to realize the greater power and usefulness of the new conception.[33]

Although these contrasting views refer primarily to science teaching, how well do you think they relate to your own teaching? To what extent will your students come with preconceptions that will conflict with what you plan to teach?

▶

Obviously, discussions of knowledge are not independent of discussions of learning. After all, "to come to know" and "to learn" are two different ways of expressing similar ideas. The distinction between the psychological term *learn* and the philosophical term *know* rests primarily on the kinds of questions the two disciplines ask regarding knowledge and its acquisition. Whereas educational psychologists investigate the actual processes through which people acquire knowledge, philosophers explore the nature, limits, and validity of knowledge, rationality, and inquiry. Therefore, it should not be surprising to find psychological theories that complement philosophical views on knowledge. Simply (or simplistically) stated, behaviorism is a modern expression of traditional empiricism, and cognitive psychology (particularly the work of Piaget, Kohlberg, and modern information-processing theorists such as Donald Norman) is consistent with a "conceptual change" viewpoint.

Not only do philosophical orientations relate to psychological theories, they also have sociological dimensions. We have already seen that knowledge to the sociologists may be considered a means of control (see pp. 47–50). Berlak and Berlak point out additional sociological dimensions of knowledge. They suggest that the traditional philosophical distinction between knowledge viewed as "given" (e.g., in realism) versus knowledge viewed as "problematic" (e.g., in experimentalism) has significant sociological implications:

Patterns that are predominantly *given* would, we suppose, convey unquestioning reverence and respect for the public knowledge transmitted by society through its agents, and ultimately for the society and its institutions as well, while heavily *problematic* patterns would convey a disposition towards criticism and analysis, of culture and society, and encourage creativity.[34]

Further, they suggest that teachers may view knowledge differently for different types of learners (see the issue of "diversity") and for different subjects. If knowledge as given (e.g., emphasizing facts) underlies our teaching of one racial, ethnic, or socioeconomic status group but not others (e.g., emphasizing critical thinking), we may be implying that certain types of people should learn to criticize their culture and society and to be creative, but other types of people should learn to accept and adjust to society's institutions. Berlak and Berlak[35] also point out that knowledge in some realms (e.g., mathematics and history) is treated as given and certain, and knowledge in other realms (e.g., literature) is treated as problematical. This differential treatment might well vary from school to school and from teacher to teacher.

In your view, is the knowledge in some subject matters more certain than in others? Should some kinds of students come to view your subject matter as certain while others develop a view of it as being less certain, more problematic? How do the tests and homework that teachers give and the way in which teachers administer and mark them convey a teacher's position on this issue?
▶

## Role of the Teacher

"Be a real person." *(Carl Rogers)*

"Children don't want teachers to be their friends, they want someone to look up to." *(Common advice to new teachers)*

Many sociologists point out that schools are both agencies of socialization and bureaucratic organizations. In their attempts at socialization, they try to promote the kinds of learning and development they deem necessary for the growth of children into responsible, productive, and competent adults. For many educators, this process requires warm interpersonal relationships tailored to the uniqueness of each individual. However, as bureaucratic agencies, schools often provide impersonal and uniform treatment. Thus, sociologically speaking, there is a conflict of roles.

Will you as a teacher be formal and businesslike with your class, maintaining sufficient social distance from the learners, or will you try to be more informal and friendly? How much of a shift in roles must occur when you move from one side of the teacher's desk to the other?
▶

If you ask "experts" for their advice on these questions, you are likely to hear conflicting views. The answers seem to depend a great deal on whom you ask. For example, compare the sociologist Willard Waller with Carl Rogers. According to Waller:

> Social distance is characteristic of the personal entanglements of teachers and students. It is a necessity where the subordination of one person to another is required, for distance makes possible that recession of feeling without which the authority of another is not tolerable. . . . Between adult and child is an irreducible social distance that seems at times an impassable gulf. The distance arises from the fact that the adult has absorbed the heritage of the group, and represents therefore in some sense the man plus the wisdom of all his ancestors, whereas the child is much more the natural and uncultivated man, and from the fact that the adult has found his place in the world and the child has not. . . . To the natural distance between adult and child is added a greater distance when the adult is a teacher and the child is a student, and this distance arises mainly from the fact that the teacher must give orders to the child; they cannot know each other, for we can never know a person at whom we only peer through institutional bars. Formality arises in the teacher–pupil relationship as a means of maintaining social distance, which in turn is a means to discipline. . . . Most important of the means whereby distance is maintained . . . is that classroom procedure which defers the situation in an impersonal manner and excludes possibilities of spontaneous human interaction. This is the dry, matter-of-fact, formal procedure of the classroom, which gives nothing and asks nothing of personality, but is always directed at the highly intellectualized matter to be studied.[36]

Consider the validity of this statement as a description of the reality of classroom teaching. Maybe you can infer Waller's attitude toward formal teaching: a necessary evil, a necessary good, or neutral. It might be interesting to consider how he would respond to this excerpt from Rogers:

> What are these qualities, these attitudes, that facilitate learning? . . . Perhaps the most basic of these essential attitudes is realness or genuineness. When the facilitator is a real person, being what she is, entering into a relationship with the learner without presenting a front or a facade, she is much more likely to be effective. This means that the feelings that she is experiencing are available to her, available to her awareness, that she is able to live these feelings, be them, and able to communicate them if appropriate. It means that she comes into a direct personal encounter with the learner, meeting her on a person-to-person basis. It means that she is *being* herself, not denying herself. . . . Thus, she is a person to her students, not a faceless embodiment of a curricular requirement nor a sterile tube through which knowledge is passed from one generation to the next. . . . It is obvious that this attitudinal set, found to be effective in psychotherapy, is sharply in contrast with the tendency of most teachers to show themselves to their pupils sim-

ply as roles. It is quite customary for teachers rather consciously to put on the mask, the role, the facade of being a teacher and to wear this facade all day removing it only when they have left the school at night.[37]

Rogers's current view is consistent with many "open education" writers around 1970 in the United States, like Charles Silberman:

Informal education relieves the teacher of the terrible burden of omniscience. . . . To the formal teacher, admitting ignorance means loss of dignity. . . . In an informal classroom, by contrast, the teacher is the facilitator [note the term *facilitator* in both Rogers's and Silberman's writing] rather than the source of learning, the source being the child himself. . . . The consequence is an atmosphere in which everyone is learning together. . . . Most important, however, the free day classroom relieves the teacher of the necessity of being a timekeeper, traffic cop, and disciplinarian. In a formal classroom, a large proportion of the teacher's time and an extraordinary amount of energy are consumed simply by the need to maintain order and control. ("I cannot begin until all talking is stopped and every eye is on me!") In the informal classroom, the discipline problem withers away, in part because children are not required to sit still and be silent. . . . A[n] [informal] teacher with forty years' experience remarks, "I try to be informal. I mean, I try to make this situation as much as possible like a family group sitting around a fireplace or around a table when some question has come up and they're discussing it."[38]

Consider your own view of the Rogers/Silberman position. Are they being realistic? Perhaps the conflict between Waller's sociological and Rogers's psychotherapeutic analysis stems from a difference between a description of the ways things are and a proposal for the way things ought to be. Maybe different disciplines of knowledge (here, sociology and psychotherapy) offer different, even conflicting, perspectives on classroom teaching.

▶

More important, what is your view regarding the informal/formal issue? How informal or formal do you plan to be, and how do you plan to express your preferred role? Think about your role in terms of the sorts of clothing you plan to wear, how you will expect your students to address you, the rules for determining speaking order in the classroom (e.g., handraising), where and how you will position yourself in the classroom, how strict you will be, what you will do when one of your students tries to approach you on a personal matter (either yours or the student's), and what sort of differences there are between your in-class and out-of-class voice. Waller points out that these aspects of a teacher's behavior all affect the teacher's prestige.

▶

## School and Society

"Teaching is subversive activity." *(Neil Postman and Charles Weingartner)*

"Dare the school build a new social order?" *(George S. Counts)*

"Schools merely reproduce the social order and perpetuate its class stratifi-cations." *(various neo-Marxists)*

"Don't make waves!" *(Anon.)*

Perhaps one or more of these quotations reflects your view of teaching.

Of course, schools are for learning. They are the society's primary means for trans-mitting the cultural heritage from one generation to the next. But some sociologists notice "two other fundamental and inseparable purposes: (1) they keep lower-class students from competing equally with middle-class students, and (2) they serve to le-gitimate the political and social system."[39] Some sociologists view schooling as a "com-petitive struggle for social and economic rewards. It is essentially a tug-of-war between the middle and lower classes, with the upper classes literally above the battle."[40]

But what roles do teachers play in this process? Although our personal political posture does not necessarily influence our daily teaching practices, most of us nev-ertheless have rather deep political convictions. These convictions may affect the teaching of social studies more than the teaching of math, but it is difficult to escape the effect altogether in any teaching situation. "Either a teaching activity serves to in-tegrate children into the current social order, or it provides children with the knowl-edge, attitudes or skills to deal critically and creatively with that reality in order to im-prove it."[41] The contexts of our teaching can never be ignored for long.

The teacher is the primary political socializing agent for the child, so the teacher's political posture is crucial.

> The teacher represents *the* authoritative spokesman of society, for the teacher is usually the first model of political authority the beginning student encounters.[42]

With teachers playing such a crucial role in the socialization of learners, some so-ciologists see the political orientation of teachers as a key factor affecting the process of education:

> The conservatism apparent in teachers is best understood, perhaps, by con-sidering them as advocates of the interests of the middle class. Teachers pre-fer to do regular rather than radical things, and they do not encourage their students to participate in politics other than in the most accepted and es-

tablished fashions. This interpretation is based upon the assumption that teachers charged with the responsibilities of injecting system maintenance values into the educational subculture encourage their students to become good citizens, and in so doing, do not offer students an alternative to acceptance of the *status quo*.[43]

These sociological claims regarding the purposes of schooling and the socialization of students and teachers may strike you as obvious or as absurd. Even if you accept these claims as valid, you may either applaud or deplore schools and teachers that serve these functions.

How do you see yourself in relation to the school and society? How politically conservative are you? How comfortable are you with people of more radical political persuasion? To what extent do you believe that the school is the *cause* of social inequalities? How supportive of "middle-class" values are you? For example, to what extent do you agree with each of the following middle-class beliefs:

1. A person's career is the most important determinant of status in our society.
2. My children should have the same educational opportunities as I have had.
3. A "good" school is one that is academically oriented.
4. Education is the pathway to economic achievement.

▶

Another way to assess your own political posture as a teacher is to consider classroom problems: Are the problems you face as a teacher basically educational problems solvable through educational means? Or do most of the problems require structural changes in schools and society? Clearly, an affirmative answer to this last question reflects a less conservative view. Although the terms *conservative* and *progressive* have recently acquired many new and misleading connotations, they still denote two ends of a continuum that describes these basic issues.

From a philosophical point of view, this issue could be treated as a debate between reconstructionists and conservatives, between philosophers such as Theodore Brameld and William Bagley:

[Brameld] While repudiating nothing of the constructive achievements of other educational theories, reconstructionism commits itself, first of all, to the renascence of modern culture. It is infused with a profound conviction that we are in the midst of a revolutionary period out of which should emerge nothing less than the control of the industrial system, of public services, and of cultural and natural resources by and for the common people who, throughout the ages, have struggled for a life of security, decency, and peace for themselves and their children.[44]

[Bagley] The very time to avoid chaos in the schools is when something akin to chaos characterizes the social environment. . . . The very time to emphasize in the schools the values that are relatively certain and stable is when the social environment is full of uncertainty and when standards are crumbling. Education follows, it does not lead. If education is to be a stabilizing force it means that the school must discharge what is in effect a disciplinary function. The materials of instruction, the methods of teaching, and the life of the school as a social organization must exemplify *and idealize* consideration, cooperation, cheerfulness, fidelity to duty and to trust, courage and perseverance in the face of disappointment, aggressive effort toward doing the task that one's hand finds to do and doing it as well as one can, loyalty to friend and family and those for whom one is responsible, a sense of fact and a willingness to face facts, clear and honest thinking. These may not be eternal values, but one may venture a fairly confident prediction that they will be just as significant a thousand years from now as they have ever been in the past.[45]

You might examine whether we are "in the midst of a revolutionary period," how "stable" our values are, and whether education follows or leads the society. What is your position regarding the reconstructionist–conservative debate, and how would your position affect your conduct as a teacher?
▶

## INTERRELATIONS AMONG THE SIX ISSUES

As with most things in education, these six issues are highly interrelated. Beliefs about learning and motivation relate directly to beliefs about knowledge, the teacher's role, and control. For example, a person with a belief in cooperative learning environments (*learning*) might be likely to value a close relationship with pupils (*teacher role*), to base context decisions on the children's interests (*knowledge* and *motivation*), and to let the children participate fully in setting rules for classroom operations (*control*). Such a teacher might be labeled "informal." In contrast with this teacher is one who emphasizes grades (extrinsic *motivation*) and, perhaps, competition (*learning*), teaches mostly facts without worrying too much about how they relate to children's past experience (*knowledge*), sets rules of conduct, and enforces them strictly but fairly (*control*) in a businesslike manner (*teacher role*). This teacher might be labeled "formal."

Labels such as formal/informal, traditional/progressive, and authoritarian/democratic might work well for extremes in teacher perspectives, but the vast majority of teachers' perspectives are too complex for such oversimplifications. Although our beliefs on one issue relate to our beliefs on another, the relationship is not entirely predictable. For example, a teacher who tries to develop a "good group" might have a self-image of a strong group leader, even as a benevolent dictator.[46] This emphasis on the group can lead to the teacher's exerting strong control of classroom behavior, being particularly strict with "uncooperative" behaviors.

Each of the six issues is far too general for use to resolve in any definitive manner. The questions used to present them can be answered similarly: "It all depends!" Actually it all depends on the four common features we discussed earlier. It all depends on who the *teacher* is; who the *learners* are; what the *subject matter* is; and in what grade level, type of school, and community (i.e., *context*) the teaching is situated. Let us examine an example of the way the resolution of basic issues depends on what the subject matter is, who the learners are, what the context is, and who the teacher is.

Mrs. Borden[47] has definite views about *subject matter,* but her views differ for each subject. She monitors the morning's work in the three Rs much more closely than she does the afternoon activities—arts and crafts, music, and dramatic play. For the three Rs she keeps careful records of both time spent and accomplishments. She treats the arts, creative play, and social development more as rewards for work in the basics than as significant subjects in their own right. Social studies and science are learned through project work in which the pupils are allowed to choose their topics.

When we look at the differential treatment of *learners* in addition to subject matter, Mrs. Borden's resolution of the issues becomes striking, particularly with regard to the consequences of her practices for her pupils. Her "slower" pupils are those who cannot quickly memorize written words and/or have not acquired decoding skills. These pupils receive more step-by-step, less broad, more extrinsically motivated, less personally relevant instruction. For example, they spend more time memorizing words out of context and more time reading from books that control vocabulary in terms of structurally similar words (e.g., *hat, cat, mat,* etc.). Perhaps because these stories lack any interest value (and, therefore, intrinsic motivation), these "slower" children are constantly pushed to "get on with it." Because some of these children come from backgrounds somewhat different from those of the other children, the content of all the instruction is less likely to relate to the life they experience after school hours and beyond the school's walls.

At the *context* of the teaching shifts, so too will the teacher's resolution of the issues. As these "slower" children move up in grade level, they may spend more time being "remediated," receiving more extrinsic motivation and less meaningful and interesting content from their remedial reading *teacher,* who may increasingly treat them as clients. Meanwhile, their "regular" teachers are likely to exert far greater control over their "faster" classmates. Many aspects of this differential treatment could be accentuated if these pupils are from low-SES neighborhoods and if the teacher is middle class and unfamiliar with low-SES people.

## SUMMARY

Notice the terrain we have traveled in this chapter. Our discussion of *control* centered on a sociological analysis of rules, socialization, and the curriculum. However, at the end of this section we mentioned psychological and philosophical dimensions of control. We discussed behavioral and cognitive psychological dimensions of *learning* and *motivation.* We viewed the *diversity of learners* from a predominantly sociological perspective, on labeling and grouping people, though the labels themselves derive from both sociology and psychology. Whether knowledge is certain or problematic was the focus of our philosophical treatment of the *knowledge* issue, though we also analyzed knowledge as a sociological issue. When we discussed the *role of the teacher,* we compared one sociological view of social distance with one psychological view of genuineness. Our discussion of *school* and *society* included the socialization of teachers and students and a comparison between two philosophies, reconstructionism and conservatism.

Obviously, each of the six issues serves as a focal point for a divergent set of foundational perspectives. The foundations of education help us raise questions and supply concepts for thinking about our own teaching practices. But the foundations cannot answer these questions. Answers reflect our own personal perspective on teaching, which in turn depend on the situation in which we teach. In order to answer these questions, we must make a commitment to a view on what good teaching is and on what a good teacher does in a particular situation.

## NOTES

1. Because of limited space, this book discusses only three of the disciplines: philosophy, psychology, and sociology.
2. These six issues are derived from the work of Ann Berlak and Harold Berlak, *Dilemmas of Schooling* (New York: Methuen, 1981).
3. Willard Waller, *The Sociology of Teaching* (New York: Wiley, 1932).
4. Robert Arnove, "On Sociological Perspective and Educational Problems," in *Education and American Culture,* eds. Elizabeth Steiner, Robert Arnove, and B. Edward McClellan (New York: Macmillan, 1980), p. 6.
5. Emile Durkheim, *Education and Sociology,* trans. Sherwood Fox (Glencoe, Ill.: Free Press, 1956).
6. Talcott Parsons, "The School Class as a Social System," *Harvard Educational Review* 29 (Fall 1959), pp. 297–318.
7. Samuel Bowles and Herbert Gintis, *Schooling in Capitalist America: Educational Reform and the Contradictions of Economic Life* (New York: Basic Books, 1976).
8. Waller, *Sociology of Teaching.*
9. Parsons, "The School Class."
10. Philip Jackson, *Life in Classrooms* (New York: Holt, Rinehart and Winston, 1968).
11. I borrowed this last point from Jane Martin, "What Should We Do with a Hidden Curriculum When We Find One?", in *The Hidden Curriculum and Moral Education,* eds. Henry Giroux and David Purpel (Berkeley, Calif.: McCutchan, 1983).
12. Jean Anyon, "Social Class and the Hidden Curriculum of Work," in *Curriculum and Instruction,* eds. Henry Giroux, Anthony Penna, and William Pinar (Berkeley, Calif.: McCutchan, 1981).
13. Ronald Corwin, *Militant Professionalism: A Study of Organizational Conflict in High Schools* (New York: Appleton, 1970), p. 234.
14. Basil Bernstein, "On the Classification and Framing of Educational Knowledge," in *Knowledge and Control: New Directions for the Sociology of Knowledge,* ed. Michael Young (London: Collier-Macmillan, 1971).
15. Max Weber, *Essays in Sociology,* trans. and eds. H. Gerth and C. W. Mills (London: Routledge and Kegan Paul, 1952).

16. A. Gramsci, *The Modern Prince and Other Writings* (translation) (New York: Monthly Review Press, 1957).

17. Michael Young, ed., *Knowledge and Control: New Directions for the Sociology of Education* (London: Collier-Macmillan, 1971), p. 36.

18. Ibid.

19. Ibid., p. 38.

20. See, for example, Kenneth Strike, *Liberty and Learning* (Oxford, England: Martin Robertson, 1982).

21. Much of this section is adapted from Thomas Good and Jere Brophy, *Educational Psychology: A Realistic Approach,* 2nd ed. (New York: Holt, Rinehart and Winston, 1980).

22. Cited by S. H. Erlwanger, "Benny's Conception of Rules and Answers in IPI Mathematics," *Journal of Children's Mathematical Behavior* 1(2) (Autumn 1973), pp. 71-90.

23. Good and Brophy, *Educational Psychology,* pp. 210-211.

24. Ibid.

25. Ibid., p. 212.

26. David Johnson and Roger Johnson, "Instructional Goal Structure: Cooperative, Competitive or Individualistic," *Review of Educational Research* 44(2) (1974), p. 218.

27. Van Cleve Morris, *Philosophy and the American School* (Boston: Houghton Mifflin, 1961).

28. Ibid.

29. See Kenneth Strike and George Posner, "Epistemological Perspectives on Conceptions of Curriculum Organization and Learning," in *Review of Research in Education,* ed. Lee Shulman, Vol. 4 (Itasca, Ill.: F. E. Peacock, 1976); Harold Brown, *Perception, Theory and Commitment: The New Philosophy of Science* (Chicago: University of Chicago Press, 1977).

30. This discussion is based on Edward Smith and Charles Anderson, "The Effects of Teacher's Guides on Teacher Planning and Classroom Instruction in Activity-Based Science." Paper presented at the Annual Meeting of the American Educational Research Association, Montreal, April 1983.

31. Ibid., p. 19.

32. Smith and Anderson (ibid.) refer to this view as the "conceptual change" view.

33. Ibid., p. 19.

34. Ann Berlak and Harold Berlak, *Dilemmas of Schooling: Teaching and Social Change* (New York: Methuen, 1981), p. 148.

35. Ibid.

36. Waller, *Sociology of Teaching,* pp. 279-280.

37. Carl Rogers, *Freedom to Learn for the 80's* (Columbus, Ohio: Charles E. Merrill, 1983), pp. 121-122.

38. Charles Silberman, *Crisis in the Classroom: The Remaking of American Education* (New York: Random House, 1970), pp. 267-271.

39. Joseph Scimecca, *Education and Society* (New York: Holt, Rinehart and Winston, 1980), p. 24.

40. Ibid., p. 24.

41. Carl Grant and Kenneth Zeichner, "On Becoming a Reflective Teacher," in *Preparing for Reflective Teaching,* ed. Carl A. Grant (Boston: Allyn and Bacon, 1984), p. 15.

42. Scimecca, *Education and Society,* p. 105.

43. Harmon Zeigler, *The Political Life of American Teachers* (Englewood Cliffs, N.J.: Prentice-Hall, 1967), pp. 21-22.

44. Theodore Brameld, adapted from *Education for the Emerging Age* (New York: Harper and Brothers, 1969), pp. 26-27.

45. William Bagley, *Education and Emergent Man* (New York: Ronald Press Co., 1934), pp. 154–156.
46. See Valerie Janesick, "An Ethnographic Study of a Teacher's Classroom Perspective," unpublished doctoral dissertation, Michigan State University, 1977.
47. A fictitious teacher inspired by several teachers described in Berlak and Berlak, *Dilemmas.*

# chapter 6

# Contributions of Methods Courses

Just as we examined the contributions of your foundational studies to your own perspective on teaching in the last chapter, we now turn to the ideas that you have learned or will learn in your study of teaching methods. The study of teaching methods is quite diverse. Few generalizations can be made about what people study in methods courses. For the purpose of using these studies as a focus for reflection on teaching, we will examine three aspects of teaching methods: lesson planning, instructional activities, and curriculum emphasis.

## LESSON PLANNING

The first issue to address regarding planning your methods of teaching is the extent to which planning is either necessary or appropriate at this point. Let's assume that your field experience consists in tutoring a sixth grader who is having trouble with her social studies. Obviously, before the first meeting any lesson planning would be pointless. However, even after meeting her and discussing the kinds of help she needs, it still may be inappropriate to plan. If your weekly meeting is to help her with her homework, to go over her weekly quiz, and to answer whatever questions she may have, planning may still be inappropriate. It all depends on the role you are being asked to play.

Suppose, on the other hand, that this sixth grader is getting poor grades, that you and she decide that she needs help preparing for the weekly quiz, and that your weekly session will be used for that purpose. In this case it is your responsibility to plan the session for this purpose, even if your plans occasionally are set aside in order to deal with problems she brings to the session.

This section of the chapter is about planning lessons. If you find in your field placement that you cannot anticipate what the learners will need, then you might not want to invest much time in planning. In any case, you might still find the material in this chapter useful, because at some point in your field experience you will likely need to plan a lesson.

## Planning Frames

Take the time now to jot down some preliminary plans for your first (or next) session in the field. Start wherever it feels comfortable. Don't worry about the form that your plan takes or about the "correctness" of it.[1]

▶

Now let us reflect on your preliminary plan. When teachers begin to plan a lesson, they typically begin with a search for an answer to one or more questions:

1. What do I want the learners to learn?
2. What should I have the learners do?
3. How much time do I need to plan for?
4. What materials will I need?
5. What content should I cover?
6. What will they do and what will I do?
7. What products, responses, reactions, and results do I want to be the consequence of the lesson?
8. What do the learners already know and what kinds of experiences have they already had?

In other words, planning typically begins with a particular concern that focuses the teacher's attention on some aspect of planning:

1. Objectives
2. Activities
3. Time
4. Materials
5. Content
6. Procedures
7. Consequences
8. Prior knowledge and experience

Each of these elements can be considered a mental structure, termed a "frame," that constitutes a functional unit guiding the teacher's thinking. In this case, the thinking consists of planning a lesson and the frame is thus called a "planning frame."[2] Although methods courses typically teach that planning should begin with one item from this list (most likely, objectives), in reality teachers begin with different planning frames, although they eventually give some consideration to all of the questions listed previously. Elementary teachers are more likely to begin with an activities frame, whereas high school teachers are more likely to begin with a content frame. Middle school teachers might begin with either of these two frames.

But, before we get locked into an overly simplistic interpretation of teacher planning, we should mention some other factors affecting choice of planning frame. Subject matter also affects the frame a teacher utilizes in planning. Some subject matter is more loaded with facts (e.g., history), lending itself to a content frame, whereas other subject matter is more experiential (e.g., physical education), lending itself to activity, procedure, and materials frames. Other factors related to the particular situation also affect the choice of an initial planning frame. Teaching a group of children with special interests (e.g., computers) or needs (e.g., non-English speaking) might lead to a planning frame that focuses on their special interests or one focusing on their needs, respectively. Planning for a tightly organized lesson to be given within a precise period of time (e.g., a 43-minute period) might lead to planning that begins by asking the question "How should I break up this time period so that my lesson has a well-defined introduction, main body, and conclusion?" (a time frame). The variations are endless.

As suggested in the previous examples of various initial planning frames, the planning frame chosen as the starting point is indicative of a particular *perception* of a situation; a planning frame does not imply an inherent property of a school, classroom, or school subject. It is possible to conceive of high schools that are not more content centered than elementary schools; in fact, there are both notable historical and contemporary examples of problem-centered, interdisciplinary high schools.[3] History is not inherently more factual than other subjects. What we typically conceive of as history taught in schools, however, seems to be quite factual. What we conceive of as a special interest or need that should be addressed, others might not. What I perceive as 43 minutes that need to be allocated, someone else might perceive as an undefined period of time during which some interesting activities can be launched, but not completed.

Therefore, choice of an initial planning frame may suggest how a teacher perceives a situation and, thus, provide an opportunity to reflect on that teacher's assumptions about teaching.

## Preliminary Plans

Examine your preliminary plans. What was your initial planning frame? That is, which of the eight questions listed were you attempting to answer?

▶

What assumptions underlie this choice of a starting point in planning? More specifically, does the choice of a particular planning frame suggest any assumptions about schools, the subject matter, the learners, or your role as the teacher? Write down your thoughts on this matter.

▶

## INSTRUCTIONAL ACTIVITIES

Eventually planning for teaching requires the choice of some set of activities. These activities range from those that are highly teacher centered, such as lectures and demonstrations, to those that are highly learner centered, such as individual project work and cooperative learning groups.

---

### EXERCISE 6.1　Assessment of Activities

Courses on teaching methods provide students with a variety of activities that a teacher can use. Whether or not you have already taken such a course, now is the time to take stock of what you know about these activities by comparing them on the basis of their strengths, weaknesses, and for whom and what they are appropriate. In addition to making an attempt at an objective assessment of activities (though no assessment is every really objective), add a blatantly subjective element to this assessment. Indicate the extent to which each relevant activity is appropriate for your own personality and style as a teacher. If any of these activities are unfamiliar to you, you might want to look them up in a general methods text.

| Activity | Strengths | Weaknesses | Learners | Goals | Appropriateness to My Personality |
|---|---|---|---|---|---|
| Lecture/demo | | | | | |
| Discussion | | | | | |
| Worksheets | | | | | |
| Cooperative learning | | | | | |
| Individual projects | | | | | |
| Group projects | | | | | |
| Role playing | | | | | |
| Simulations/ games | | | | | |
| Debates | | | | | |
| Field trips | | | | | |
| Laboratories | | | | | |
| Films/tapes/ slides | | | | | |
| Other | | | | | |

## CURRICULUM EMPHASIS[4]

Every time we teach a subject we give it a particular emphasis. For example, if we teach science, we might find our lessons aimed at one or more of the following emphases:

1. Students must learn how to apply scientific principles to our technological and natural environment. (Coping with problems)
2. Students must engage in real scientific inquiry themselves, during which time they examine the interplay between theory and evidence, the adequacy of particular models used to explain physical phenomena, and the tentativeness of scientific knowledge. (Structure of science)
3. Science is viewed as a set of skills to be learned rather than as knowledge to be acquired, i.e., process rather than product oriented. (Scientific skill development)
4. Clear explanations by teachers and acceptance of ideas by students. (Transmission of cultural heritage)
5. Mastery of content. (Provision of solid foundation)
6. Science education examines the growth and change in scientific ideas as a function of human purposes and historical settings. (Science as a cultural institution)

After each emphasis listed I have attempted to summarize the justification (in parentheses) a teacher might propose for teaching science. As you can see, a particular emphasis is based on a particular justification for teaching that subject matter. It should be clear that none of these emphases is correct or incorrect. Each might be "right" in a particular situation—that is, with particular learners—in a particular setting and with a particular teacher.

In addition, your personal history (see Chapter 4) has contributed greatly to the particular emphases you are likely to give to the various subject matters you will teach. If you are preparing to teach a particular subject matter (e.g., English), these two factors probably even contributed to your decision to teach this subject matter in the first place.

---

### EXERCISE 6.2  Justifying Subject Matter

In your fieldwork you may be responsible for teaching particular subject matters or topics. If this is the case, choose one for which you have been given the greatest degree of autonomy. For this subject matter or topic try to generate a set of (three to five) possible answers to the following question:

Why study this subject matter or topic? Do not worry if your answers overlap slightly.

▶

Now, for each justification, try to describe a particular emphasis that is consistent with the justification.

▶

Finally, write a statement describing the justification and emphasis that you believe underlies your teaching at your particular field placement.

▶

## THEORY AND PRACTICE

Most methods courses present more than the nuts and bolts of teaching. They also represent a particular set of beliefs about teaching. In your methods courses you might have focused on the teaching practices. Here we focus on the underlying beliefs. For example, on the surface, Reading Recovery is a program designed for students in early primary school who are at risk of educational failure. It attempts to teach a set of reading strategies based on what the child already knows using a basic lesson format. At the same time, Reading Recovery is also a set of beliefs about learning. These beliefs include the following: (1) Each child is an active learner; (2) children bring their own meaning to the books they read; (3) good readers use particular strategies that weak readers can learn; (4) children learn to use multiple sources of information whenever they read or write. Notice that these beliefs all focus on the basic issue of learning.

Other topics in methods courses might focus on other issues. The six issues presented in Chapter 5 can function as a useful road map for charting the beliefs of each topic presented in your methods courses. You should be able to relate each topic to one or more of these basic issues. For example, multicultural education focuses on issues related to both diversity and the relation between school and society, whereas assertive discipline focuses on issues of control and the role of the teacher. By way of contrast, constructivist methods of teaching mathematics and science focus on issues related to both knowledge and learning.

### EXERCISE 6.3   Identifying Issues

Take stock of the topics presented in your methods courses. For as many as possible, identify which of the six issues presented in Chapter 5 relate most directly to the beliefs underlying the topic. Then, specifically identify as many of the underlying beliefs as you can for each of these topics.

Here is a list of possible topics. Some items were not included in your particular methods courses. And, no doubt, there were topics you encountered that are not on this list. Use the list only as a point of departure for this exercise.

Whole language
Constructivism
Multicultural education
Process writing
Cooperative learning
Discovery learning
Individualized instruction
Mastery learning
Behavioral objectives
Portfolio assessment
Other topics

## NOTES

1. Edward L. Smith and Neil B. Sendelbach, "The Programme, the Plans and the Activities of the Classroom: The Demands of Activity-based Science," in *Innovation in the Science Curriculum,* ed. John Olson (London: Croon Helm, 1982).
2. Ibid., pp. 101–105.
3. See Lawrence A. Cremin, *The Transformation of the School* (New York: Alfred A. Knopf, 1961) for historical examples.
4. Adapted from Douglas Roberts, "Developing the Concept of 'Curriculum Emphasis' in Science Education," *Science Education* 60(2) (1982), 243–260.

# chapter 7

# Initial Perspective

*A thoughtful man is neither the prisoner of his environment nor the victim of his biography.*[1]

It always seems difficult to take a stand, to make a commitment. Maybe that is why people try to avoid taking a position on basic issues. But when you devote the time and energy and take the risks involved in formulating your views, you lay the groundwork for personal and professional growth. By making your perspective on teaching explicit, you can become a more reflective teacher, less likely to be a slave to your unexamined assumptions and more open to change based on your daily experiences.

In previous chapters you analyzed the situation in which you will teach and examined your past experiences and foundational studies as sources for a perspective on teaching. This chapter helps you to sort out your ideas about teaching and to come to terms with your current perspective.

## SORTING OUT IDEAS

In Chapter 11 you will examine the cooperating teacher's perspective. Perhaps you will find yourself agreeing with the cooperating teacher. But maybe you would do things differently if you were in charge. An important part of your growth as a teacher will result from your examination of your beliefs about teaching.

One way to sort out ideas is to react to a set of assertions about teaching. Your reactions will help you examine your beliefs on teaching. These beliefs, taken as a whole, constitute your initial perspective.

An instrument is provided in Appendix A, the Teaching Belief Inventory (TBI), designed to help you make your own beliefs about teaching more explicit. Take the time now to complete the TBI. We will use your responses to the statements in it as the basis for further work in this chapter.

## ANALYSIS OF BELIEFS

The TBI consists of 57 items grouped into the six basic issues introduced in Chapter 5. Each basic issue encompasses between 3 and 21 items in the TBI. For further study select two or three basic issues or specific aspects of basic issues. It is probably more useful to focus on a small set of issues in depth than to attempt to think through your views on a wide range of issues. In order to make this selection, you might examine your responses to groups of items.

▶ Which groups of items (i.e., issues) were most relevant to your field experience and, therefore, elicited some response?

▶ To which groups of items or issues were your responses most extreme (i.e., a response of 1 or 4)?

▶ To which groups of items or issues did you give a qualified response (i.e., a response of 2 or 3)?

▶ Which issues concern you most?

▶ With this analysis of your responses in mind, you can decide now on which two or three issues you would like to focus your inquiry and explain the reasons behind your choice.

Now you can examine your response to the groups of items you just selected and summarize and elaborate your responses to form a coherent answer to a selected subset of the following questions:

1. Control
   a. How should classroom procedures be determined? (Items 1-5)
   b. How should curriculum and content be determined? (Items 6-15)
   c. How much input should the teachers and parents have regarding the administration of the school? (Items 16-18)
   d. How much control should teachers have over learners' behavior? (Items 19-21)

   ▶

2. Diversity
   a. How should learners' differences be handled? (Items 22-29)

   ▶

3. Learning
   a. Is learning facilitated by an individualistic, competitive, or cooperative environment? (Items 30-32)
   b. How does one acquire competence in a subject matter? (Items 33-35)
   c. What is the basis for motivation? (Items 36-37)

   ▶

4. Teacher's role
   a. How formal a role should the teacher assume? (Items 38-40)

   ▶

5. School and society
   a. How active should the teacher become in reforming the school and the society? (Items 41-45)
   b. Are schools the cause of social inequalities or are school problems merely the effects of these societal problems? (Items 46-47)

   ▶

6. Knowledge
   a. What should be the curriculum's emphasis? (Items 48-55)
   b. Should different subject matters be kept separate or integrated? (Items 56-57)

   ▶

For the purpose of future discussions, your responses to the Teacher Belief Inventory, together with your summary and elaboration of those responses focusing on two or three issues, constitute what we shall call your "initial perspective on teaching." This perspective is not a general philosophy of teaching but a set of beliefs regarding your specific field experience.

## TRACING ORIGINS

We are obviously not born with perspectives on teaching. Where do they come from? By tracing our beliefs back to their origins, we are in a better position to examine their validity. The beliefs become less taken for granted as we identify their sources. We have discussed some of the sources for a perspective in Chapters 4, 5, and 6. Reread your analyses of your experiences as a learner and as a teacher (Chapter 4).

To what extent have these past experiences affected your initial perspective? What other significant experiences have made an impact on your perspective? In what ways?

▶

Did your family's attitude toward teaching or toward education influence your perspective? What about the way you or your brothers and sisters were treated as children by your parents?

▶

What about your professional training? Have the values expressed by faculty members or by your fellow students influenced your perspective? In what ways?

▶

## CONSIDERING CONSEQUENCES

The saying "actions speak louder than words" might well have been written to describe the effects of teaching. Any teacher's perspective, if implemented, has consequences for learners. Teachers act in certain ways based on their beliefs and on contextual constraints, and learners interpret the teacher's actions in both intended and unintended ways. The unintended meanings learners derive from a teacher's actions are part of the school's "hidden curriculum"[2] discussed in Chapter 5. For example, a female teacher in a working-class community school keeps a tight control over pupils' classroom behavior, requiring permission before any learner may speak and keeping all children in their seats except when she gives them bathroom passes. She presents the subject matter through a lecture-recitation method, emphasizing rote memorization of the facts as she or the textbook presents them. The children are always kept busy in class, and their homework consists of worksheets with detailed instructions to follow. Promptness, neatness, effort, and compliance with instructions are highly emphasized. The teacher makes a point of publicly displaying the individual pupil's work that most successfully meets these criteria.

Another female teacher works in a school whose community is dominated by the research and development (R&D) division of a large electronics corporation. She allows a great deal of movement in her classroom: Children speak to her and to their classmates without raising hands; different activities are located around the room with children moving from one to another at will; children leave the room to visit the bathroom or learning center without passes. Most of the children engage either in projects during class time with the teacher acting as a resource person, or in small discussion sessions with the teacher acting as a facilitator. Children actively question and criticize sources of information and learn to derive their own conclusions from the available evidence. Independent and logical thinking, problem-solving ability, and creativity seem to be what this teacher looks for in the children's work. Children are encouraged to work cooperatively on the projects they select together and the teacher tries to use inherent interest in projects as the primary motivation.

What might be the differences between the messages that pupils in these two different classrooms receive?

▶

Now apply a similar analysis to your own initial perspective. Try to identify the messages or meanings the learners are likely to take from your beliefs if and when you implement them.[3] Consider both intended and unintended meanings, both short- and long-term effects.

The following sets of questions illustrate this approach to the analysis of your initial perspective for possible consequences. They are only examples. They are grouped according to the same issues presented in Chapter 5 and used to organize the Belief Inventories in Appendix A.

- *Diversity of Learners.* Would you treat different groups of learners differently? Would this differential treatment affect any groups' ability or desire to assume particular social roles in the future?
- *Learning.* Would your emphasis be on the kind of motivation that grades or personal recognition generate, or on the inherent interest learners derive from work they choose to do? What would be the likelihood of the learners' motivation continuing beyond the school years and outside the school walls? How would the learners likely view the subject matter you teach?
- *Role of Teacher and Control.* What views on authority would the learners likely derive from your role as a teacher and the patterns of control you develop? Would they view authority as arbitrary or reasonable, based on power or on competence, absolute or negotiable?
- *School and Society.* From the example you set for the learners, would they

be inclined to attempt to change the social order or try to adjust to it? Would they be inclined to participate actively in the political process or to allow others to do it for them? Would they be inclined to acquiesce to authority or to assess independently the validity of claims?

- *Knowledge.* Would the learners be inclined to view school subject matter as absolute or tentative, value neutral or value laden, useful for interpreting their own everyday experience or primarily for academic matters, comprehensible as an integrated whole or as a set of compartmentalized subjects or topics within subjects?

Although questions such as these are difficult for you to answer before having had a great deal of teaching experience, jot down any answers you can give to any of these questions.

▶

Reread your responses in this section. Do they cause you to reconsider any aspects of your perspective? Write down any reservations you now have about your perspective.

▶

## GOALS

Chapter 2 discussed the goals or priorities you set for yourself as a *student* teacher. This section will help you use your thinking about your perspective to develop the goals or priorities that you, as a student *teacher*, set for your learners. These latter goals will serve as a guide to your teaching.

### Are Goals Necessary?

Education is a purposeful activity. If it has no direction, then it is unlikely to be successful. Without direction, it is even difficult to decide what should count as success.

The same can be said of teaching. One of the major differences between teaching and other interpersonal interactions, such as baby-sitting, is that teaching has direction. If someone is unable or unwilling to guide an interaction toward some growth or learning, then it is not proper to call that interaction "teaching." Field experiences can be found in many sites: schools, 4-H, Boy Scouts, Girl Scouts, nursing homes, prison, Big Brother/Big Sister programs, and many more. Whether they count as "teaching" field experiences depends on the appropriateness of someone giving direction or guidance to the interpersonal interaction. In schools, everybody expects the teacher to take responsibility for the learning of the students. In other settings, people may expect or want some degree of "teaching." On the other hand, the situation may call only for a person to be someone's friend or to keep someone company.

To force "teaching" on someone who does not want it in a situation that does not call for it or to avoid the teacher's role when the situation requires it are both common faults of students beginning their initial field experiences. Students do not always give the appropriate amount of direction to the interactions they have with their clients or pupils.

## What Are Some Tentative Goals?

Your initial perspective has already touched on many issues related to goals. By formulating your initial statement of perspective you were, in part, setting goals for your teaching.

Each dimension—that is, each of the six basic issues—is related to goals of teaching. Each issue raises questions about goals that your perspective might have addressed. By revisiting your perspective you might gain another basis for revising or expanding your goals.

***Control.*** Who really sets the goals, and who do you think should: the administration, textbook publishers, the state, the cooperating teacher, or you? How sensitive should you be to learner interests?
▶

***Diversity.*** Should you apply the same goals to all the learners regardless of their backgrounds or abilities?
▶

***Teacher's Role.*** Is it important for the learners to develop certain attitudes or feelings toward you as the teacher, such as trust, respect, or honesty?
▶

***Learning.*** Is it important for you to develop a sense of group identity? Should cooperative, competitive, or individualist attitudes be developed? Should you try to develop an interest in the subject matter, and how important is this interest? Should you try to develop a sense of the whole, or should the emphasis be on a set of building blocks of knowledge skills?
▶

***Knowledge.*** What is more important to learn: process-type knowledge (such as inquiry, problem solving, and creativity) or content-type knowledge (such as facts, concepts, and principles)? Should you help learners to construct their own interpretation of the content or to learn the "accepted" view? Do you want learners to view knowledge as certain or as tentative?

▶

*School and Society.* Are you trying to help the learners adjust to or integrate into the current social order or to provide them "with the knowledge, attitudes, or skills to deal critically and creatively with that reality in order to improve it"?[4]

▶

If you have not done so up to this point, state your goals for the field experience. What do you want to accomplish? In what ways do you intend the field experience to benefit the learner(s)?

## Reviewing Goals

You might want to review your goals. For example, you could do the following exercises:

1. Determine if they are realistic. Can you implement them in this school with this cooperating teacher?

▶

2. Sort them into short- and long-term goals. For each long-term goal, you could make sure you also have something immediate at which to aim. For each short-term goal, decide if it is an end in itself or a means to an end. If the latter case applies, what is the ultimate end? Was this end included as one of your goals?

▶

3. For each goal try to identify one or two sample indicators (i.e., things to look for that indicate the goal is achieved).

▶

4. Next to each goal write 1, 2, or 3 to indicate the priority you assign to it. Let 1 signify that the goal is essential and that you would consider your teaching a failure if it were not largely achieved. Let 2 signify that the goal is very important but that you still would consider your teaching worthwhile for the

pupils even if you achieve only partial success toward this goal. Let 3 signify that the goal would be nice to achieve but is far from essential. Your success as a teacher does not depend on your success with this goal. Now you might want to write down your 1-rated goals here. These will receive the highest priority in your field experience.

▶

Having considered your goals in terms of feasibility, long- and short-term implications, indicators of achievement, and priorities, you might find it necessary to make revisions. If so, do it here.

▶

The goals you have set are only tentative. As you proceed in your field experience, you will undoubtedly have to make midcourse corrections. Goals that initially seem to be straightforward and clearly important may need to be modified or replaced. For example, a learner's math problem may turn out to be a motivational problem, and the teacher would have to adjust goals accordingly.

Not only should goals be modified when necessary; they should also be suspended at times. You should expect to encounter situations in which your goals have to be put aside while you deal with other more pressing problems or capitalize on opportune moments. For example, a teacher may want to postpone teaching how to analyze a poem if the learners just experienced a violent situation in the school, watched a controversial television program, or are excited about an upcoming election.

Goals can guide teaching without placing a stranglehold on it. The key is flexibility in their selection and use.

## NOTES

1. George Kelly, *The Psychology of Personal Constructs,* Vol. 2 (New York: W. W. Norton, 1955), p. 560.
2. Philip Jackson, *Life in Classrooms* (New York: Holt, Rinehart and Winston, 1968).
3. Carl Grant and Kenneth Zeichner, "On Becoming a Reflective Teacher," in *Preparing for Reflective Teaching,* ed. Carl A. Grant (Boston: Allyn and Bacon, 1984), p. 15.
4. Ibid.

# part III
# What Is the Situation Where You Will Teach?

# chapter **8**

# The Community and the School

**M**ost people approach social situations with caution. They reserve judgment and commitment until they know something about the individuals and their expectations, the social rules and procedures, and the relation between the specific situation and the larger social context. Most of these factors can be taken for granted in familiar settings, such as college courses or meetings of student activity groups, though every new course or meeting requires a bit of analysis and readjustment. For example, most students spend their first class session figuring out what their instructor expects of the students. And most freshmen in college spend the entire year figuring out how the whole place works both academically and socially.

In other words, some sort of situation analysis is a necessary part of any social interaction. Because a field experience in teaching is one sort of social interaction, it, too, requires some preliminary analysis of the setting.

This chapter and the next use two types of information for the purpose of analysis: *observations* and *conversations.* Observations can focus on any of the following: (1) the community or neighborhood in which you have your field experiences; (2) the particular school agency or institution, including the physical, social, and personal setting; (3) the room or more generally the space in which you work; (4) the curriculum into which your lessons must fit; (5) the students (or, more generally, the learners) whom you will teach; and (6) the cooperating teacher (CT) or co-workers, if any, including their lessons. In addition to observations, conversations with any of the following people could be informative: the CT or co-workers (if any); the principal or immediate supervisor of your work (if any); and the learners, clients, or members of the group or family.

If your field experience is done within a school or as a supplement to schooling (e.g., tutoring in school subjects), then you might focus your analysis on the school, the student population, the community, the cooperating teacher, and the classroom.

However, if your field experience is done within another context (e.g., a 4-H club or a correctional facility), you will have to adapt Chapters 8 to 11 to the special setting in which you will teach. In doing so, you will find ideas in these four chapters that you can modify for your purposes. For example, if you serve as a co-leader of 4-H, the other co-leader is not a cooperating teacher (CT), but much of what we discuss about CTs applies equally well to co-leaders.

This chapter focuses only on the analysis of the school and the community. The next chapter examines the classroom and the curriculum.

## THE COMMUNITY

The classroom is a society in miniature. This minisociety reflects in part the society in which the school exists. Children often act and interact in certain ways because they see their parents and friends do so. If they experience anti-intellectualism, materialism, conformity, or prejudice at home or at their neighbors' houses, they are likely to demonstrate these tendencies at school. If their parents and neighbors support the school's efforts, place a high priority on achievement, and are courteous and well mannered, the children are likely to be similarly inclined in school. It is therefore important to find out about the community from which the learners come and in which the school is situated. Although interviews with parents and community members are obviously desirable, they are typically not feasible.

---

### EXERCISE 8.1   Analysis of the Community

Here are some things you can do to learn about the community:

1. Read a local newspaper every day for a couple of weeks. Pay particular attention to news stories, editorials, and letters to the editor concerning the schools.
   a. Is the community proud of its schools? What do they seem to be most proud of? The athletic teams? The band? Scholarship winners? Innovations? Efforts to cut the budget? Improved test scores? The buildings?

   ▶

   b. What makes people angry? Liberal policies? Conservative policies? Indecision? Political heavy-handedness? Permissiveness? Vandalism?

   ▶

**c.** Read noneducation-related items. How diverse is the community? Ethnically? In terms of socioeconomic status?

▶

**d.** Where do people work and what do they spend their leisure time doing?

▶

Write a brief description of the community and its attitude toward the schools as reflected by the newspaper.

▶

2. Walk around the neighborhood of the school, looking at the houses, businesses, and people on the street. Go to a local establishment near the school building, perhaps a barber shop, restaurant, bar, or self-service laundry. If asked about yourself, mention that you will be working at the school soon and note the reaction. Sympathy? Admiration? Suspicion? Listen to conversations or start one. What do the people think about the job the schools are doing? What do they think about young people today? What is first and foremost on their minds? Property taxes? Deterioration of the neighborhood? Permissiveness? Vandalism? Busing? Write a brief description of the neighborhood, its inhabitants, and their attitude toward the schools as you find it reflected in these experiences.

▶

Perhaps the school draws students from several neighborhoods. How do these neighborhoods contrast?

▶

Compare your two descriptions. Do they conflict or do they complement one another? If they conflict, how can you reconcile them? Does the newspaper really reflect the local neighborhood? Did you read enough of it? Were you exposed to enough community members to get an accurate picture?

▶

Now try to draw some implications from this study for the school and classroom. To do this, make some predictions of what you might find in the school. What sorts of careers are likely to be most and least highly prized? How much value is likely to be placed on proper dress for the pupils and for the teachers? How cautious are the teachers likely to be with regard to discussing controversial issues in the classroom? How much support from the parents are teachers likely to get when they discipline students?

▶

## THE SCHOOL

Schools are both similar and different. Compared with hospitals and churches, schools in general are distinctive and highly uniform. But within this relative uniformity, there are significant differences or variations on a theme. And just as with faces, the more one comes to know schools, the more one becomes sensitive to the differences. Some teem with activity. Others are as hushed as libraries. Some are colorful and stimulate the senses. Others are dull and drab. In some, long, straight corridors dominate the architecture. In others, open spaces are common. Some school groups resemble country clubs whereas others resemble prisons. What accounts for the differences in atmosphere and what effect do these differences have on the people who function there?

### EXERCISE 8.2    A Walk around the School

Take a walk around the school, both inside and out (remember to have the permission of the principal). Here are some things to which you might want to pay particular attention:

1. *The halls.* Who is in the halls during class time? Teachers? The principal? Students? Do the students you find have hall passes? Where are they going?

▶

Look at the walls. Are they used for displays of any kind? If so, is it student work? Commercially prepared displays? Are they at eye level for children? What subject matter is represented? Any announcements or bulletin boards? What is on them?

▶

What is the noise level and what kind of noise is it? Laughter? Yelling? A "hum of activity"? Hammering and other construction noises? Teachers' voices?

▶

Are the halls littered? How much pride in the school is evidenced?

▶

2. *The library (learning center).* Is it an inviting place? Do you find it a comfortable environment for reading? Browsing?

What is the noise level? Hushed silence? Outbursts of laughter? Are there distractions? Is the atmosphere serious or silly? Stiff or relaxed?

What is the attitude of the teacher in charge? Does he or she act more as a resource person or as a warden?

Are students there by choice or by assignment? Do they come with or without passes? Is coming to the library viewed more as a privilege or as a necessary task?

▶

---

### EXERCISE 8.3  A Conversation with the Principal

You might get an opportunity to talk with the principal. If you do, here are some suggestions that will increase your understanding of the school and, particularly, the principal's role in it.

#### Curriculum

Ask the principal about the school's objectives and curriculum. Is there a state curriculum? Try to acquire a copy. Under what objectives does the school operate? Are there objectives that the school as a whole tries to achieve? Are there particular objectives for each grade level and/or each subject? How and by whom were these developed? Who selected the textbooks and programs in use? How were they selected?

▶

#### Multicultural Aspects

Ask the principal about the ethnic, racial, religious, and socioeconomic backgrounds of the students in the school. How diverse is the student population? What minority groups in the community seem most concerned about the school's ability to provide an appropriate education for their children? How would he or she describe the experience of minorities in the school? Can he or she think of any exceptions to this generality? What are the school's expectations for each of the minority groups? Are any of the groups under- or overrepresented in remedial classes, programs for the gifted and talented, or in the upper or lower tracks (if the school is tracked)? If so, why?

### Organization and Schedule

Ask the principal about the size of the school, the number of teachers, and the size of classes. On this last matter, ask about the average size class and the range of class sizes within the school. Ask to see a copy of the "master schedule." With this schedule in hand ask the principal or try to determine from the schedule the number of planning and preparation periods, as well as the number of nonteaching duties (e.g., cafeteria duty) for each teacher. If this is a secondary school, notice the number of preparations (i.e., different courses) for each teacher and the number of teachers in each department. This schedule will also tell you the length of each period and the number of class periods each day. Ask the principal about the number of tracks, ability groups, or levels at which courses are offered. If this is an elementary school, try to determine whether there is a schoolwide uniformity with regard to scheduling language arts and math, or if this is a matter for each teacher to determine. Notice on the schedule at what grades subjects begin to become departmentalized, that is, when students go to a different teacher for a particular subject. Ask the principal about "pull-outs." Approximately how many children in each class are "pulled out" of their regular class for special help? And how many special services are provided through the use of pull-outs? Are there any times during the day when no pull-outs occur? Are any special services provided in the regular classroom? Finally, ask the principal about ability grouping within the classrooms. How many reading groups are used at each grade level? Are any other subjects ability grouped?

▶

### Rules and Discipline

What are the school's rules and how is discipline handled? Is there a printed set of rules of conduct? If not, what are they? What infractions are the most serious and what are the penalties? What is the frequency of infractions? Who is supposed to deal with each type of infraction? When should an infraction be handled entirely within the classroom? When and how should the principal (or vice-principal) be involved? When and how should parents be involved?

▶

### Leadership Style

Try to determine from the principal's remarks if he or she is more of a manager or an instructional leader. The former tries to keep a school running smoothly and efficiently. The latter tries to stimulate innovation, to encourage thought and debate, to keep teachers' minds active, and even to set an example as a continuously growing and expanding professional. Obviously, the two types of principals have very different approaches to controversy, disruptions, noise, etc.

Clearly, the kind of teacher you are encouraged to be will differ depending on the atmosphere established by different principals.

▶

---

**EXERCISE 8.4    A Visit to the Faculty Room**

If you go to the faculty room for a cup of coffee, listen to the types of conversations going on. Here are some things to notice: How old are the teachers in the room? What subjects are discussed? Are they related or not related to school? What outside activities predominate? Sports? Politics? Social events? What school-related matters predominate? Classroom problems? Concern for particular pupils? The administration? Other teachers? Parents? School sports? When discussion is on a particular student, does the talk reflect disgust, respect, hope, or despair for the student? How do the teachers dress?

▶

At this point it might be worthwhile to summarize your conclusions about the school and its staff. What is their philosophy of teaching? Do you agree with it? What sorts of problems might you encounter working there?

▶

---

The information you have collected using this chapter as a guide will help you better understand what it might be like to teach in this school. Each school has a character of its own; some even go so far as to call it a culture.[1] Take the time to write down your conclusions from this analysis. What aspects of the community and the school are you most excited about?

▶

What aspects of the community and school have you most concerned?

▶

## NOTE

1. See Michael Fullan, *The New Meaning of Educational Change,* 2nd ed. (New York: Teacher's College Press, 1991); Seymour B. Sarason, *The Culture of the School and the Problem of Change,* 2nd ed. (Boston: Allyn and Bacon, 1982).

# chapter 9

# The Classroom and the Curriculum

As Lortie[1] mentions, "the average student has spent 13,000 hours in direct contact with classroom teachers by the time he or she graduates from high school."[2] Lortie calls this contact "apprenticeship by observation."[3] There are definite limits to this type of apprenticeship, however,

> The student is the "target" of teacher efforts and sees the teacher front stage and center like an audience viewing a play. Students do not receive invitations to watch the teacher's performance from the wings; they are not privy to the teacher's private intentions and personal reflections on classroom events. Students rarely participate in selecting goals, making preparations, or postmortem analyses. Thus they are not pressed to place the teacher's actions in a pedagogically oriented framework. They are witnesses from their own student-oriented perspectives. . . . What students learn about teaching, then, is intuitive and imitative rather than explicit and analytical; it is based on individual personalities rather than pedagogical principles.[4]

Students, then, should be expected to know no more about teaching than an avid moviegoer knows about directing or a dance buff knows about choreography. One of the tasks of this chapter will be to unlearn (but not to forget) the student perspective as one step toward becoming a teacher. As Walker and Adelman[5] state:

> The teacher sees the class quite differently from the way it is seen by a child. Children are faced with the problem of either producing a performance that the teacher requires, or reacting against it in some way. In either event, a major element in the classroom situation for the pupils is what they take to be

the demands of the teacher, whether these are stated or unstated. For them the situation is inevitably one of constraint. . . .

For the teacher the problem is quite different: his task is to get beyond the constraints as rapidly as possible; he has to define the situation and set the pace—to make sure that what he wants to happen seems to happen.

For many people starting teaching, it comes as a shock to realize that the spotlight is on them, that the initiative is in their hands, that they suddenly have responsibility for what happens, what will happen and what might happen. The classroom, which they saw previously as an unshakable social structure, suddenly becomes bewildering and problematic, fraught with difficulties at every turn. Many consequently exaggerate in their minds the degree to which the situation is "out of control" simply because they are unaware of the change in perspective brought about by the shift from the back to the front of the class.[6]

Thus, seeing the teacher and the classroom differently is the main task here. Whereas the last chapter focused on the school as a whole, this chapter examines the particular classroom or setting in which you will work. Whereas the last chapter helped you to see the school from the faculty's, the principal's, and the typical student's perspective, this chapter helps you understand what dilemmas and tasks the teacher faces and what the teacher does to cope with them. Chapter 10 helps you look at the particular students you will be teaching.

Thinking in terms of frames (mentioned in Chapter 6), you may think of the community as forming a frame within which schools operate. Schools, in turn, form another frame within which classrooms operate. Classrooms, too, form a frame within which teaching occurs, and it is that innermost frame we consider here.

## THE CLASSROOM

Teachers try to provide environments for learning. The environment includes a physical and an interpersonal dimension. In order to understand the resources and constraints within which the classroom operates and the way the classroom layout reflects the teacher's personal perspective, we will begin our analysis of the classroom by examining the physical layout.

---

### EXERCISE 9.1   Classroom Map

One way to analyze the classroom layout is to make a sketch, roughly to scale. Here are some things to include and label, if present:

1. Doors and windows
2. Desks, tables, and chairs
3. Bookcases, cabinets, and display cases

4. Closets and other storage areas
5. Sinks and lavatories
6. Adjoining rooms or hallways
7. Blackboards, projectors, screens
8. Special resource areas (e.g., math table, reading corner)

(Use a separate sheet of paper for your map.)

▶

In addition, you might want to note the following features of the classroom:

1. *Walls.* Describe color. What posters, pictures, wall charts, exhibits, or notices are there? How long have they been there? Do they look as though they are still being used by someone?

2. *Vantage point.* Do any other parts of the school overlook the room? Does the room look out on the outside world?

3. *Furniture.* Does the furniture arrangement appear more conducive to cooperative, competitive, or individualistic work? How flexible does the arrangement appear? In what condition is the furniture? Has it been abused?

4. *Equipment.* What kinds of equipment are there? How accessible is it? What condition is it in? Does it look as though it is seldom, occasionally, or frequently used? And used by whom, the teacher or the learners?

5. *Bulletin boards.* What are they used for? Who uses them (the teacher, the learners, or the administration)? How recently were they changed?

6. *Specialization.* Are there areas in the room used for special purposes? Is specialization by school subject (e.g., math area), by topic or unit (e.g., space travel), or by learning mode (e.g., audiotutorial)?

7. *Atmosphere.* Note the room's temperature, air circulation and ventilation, smells, lighting (artificial and natural) and glare, acoustics (echoes and resonance), outside noise (e.g., traffic), and furniture noise.

General comments: What are your general impressions of this room? Is it crowded, cluttered, or comfortable? Is it boring and bland, or stimulating? How would you like to spend six hours a day here? If you had not met or observed the teacher, from what you have noted about the classroom, what might you assume about the teacher's approach to teaching?

▶

## THE CURRICULUM

Using the idea of frames within frames mentioned earlier in this chapter, the curriculum functions as a frame within which teachers plan lessons. Sometimes these curricular frames are school districtwide, sometimes they are schoolwide, and occasionally they are unique to the particular classroom.

### EXERCISE 9.2   Curriculum Analysis

What you see taking place when you observe a teacher teaching a lesson is part of a larger story. Before examining one particular scene of the drama—that is, a lesson—it is useful to examine the entire script. In this way, you will gain an understanding of the teacher's reasons for choosing to teach a particular lesson in a particular way, both in terms of where the teacher is going with the lesson and where the learners have already come from. It is for this reason that some analysis of the teacher's curriculum is important as you reflect on what you see and hear in the classroom or whatever is the setting for the lesson. If there is a document that the teacher uses to guide his or her daily planning, then ask to see it. This document may or may not be called the "curriculum." It may instead be called the "syllabus," the "scope and sequence," the "leader's guide," or simply the "teacher's guide." For teachers who teach strictly by the book, you may only be able to find a textbook. Once you obtain one or more documents that the teacher uses as a basis for planning, try to answer the following questions:

1.  What seems to be the underlying philosophy that guides the general approach? You might want to refer back to the discussion of the six basic issues (Chapter 5) as a source of ideas in this inquiry. Often curriculum documents do not make their basic philosophical commitments explicit, leaving the teacher in the position of reading between the lines. The sections about learning and motivation, the role of the teacher, and knowledge will likely be the most relevant to this search for a philosophy.

2.  What appear to be the curriculum's educational goals and objectives? That is, what are the intended characteristics of learners who complete the entire curriculum? Consider both their general characteristics and more specific learning outcomes. Examples of the former include goals, such as becoming more tolerant of people who are different and becoming more scientifically and mathematically literate. Examples of the latter include knowledge and skills, such as knowing about specific contributions made by particular ethnic groups and being able to calculate the slope of a straight line graph.

3.  What seem to be the general beliefs about the best methods of teaching? Is the expected role of the teacher a transmitter of information, a group facilitator, a resource person, a source of intellectual stimulation, a coach, a social worker or counselor, a task master, or some other role? What roles are learners expected to play?

4. What does the curriculum appear to count as success in teaching and how (if at all) does the curriculum suggest that learning should be evaluated? Is success to be judged by evidence on paper-and-pencil tests or by performance of real-world tasks?

▶

### EXERCISE 9.3   Lesson Profile[7]

*Like a piece of music, a good lesson can have different "movements" which have various, contrasting moods, but which, taken together as a sequence, form a cumulative experience.*[8]

With this basic familiarity of the classroom layout, you are equipped to observe the class in action. A useful way to begin is by making a lesson profile of one or two lessons (i.e., class periods). Think of a lesson as a sequence of events; there is a beginning, a middle, and an end. The beginning might consist of a settling-down period, a preface and/or introduction, or the presentation of instructions for the main activity. The middle might entail a demonstration, lecture, film, discussion, presentation of work by groups, set work, or any combination of these and other activities. The end might be used as a period for summary, conclusions, cleaning up, homework assignments, test taking, among other things. You might list the sequence of events that took place during the lesson, indicating the approximate length of time each event required, and describing what seem to you to be important aspects of each. You might want to include information about some of the following for each event:

1. Activity of teacher (what is the teacher doing?)
2. Activity of learners (what are the learners doing?)
3. Resources (what resources are utilized?)
4. Noise level (high, moderate, low)
5. Use of space (what areas of the classroom are used?)
6. Concentration level (high, moderate, low)
7. Movement of learners
8. Movement of teacher
9. Number of learners involved
10. Lines of communication (teacher to student, student to teacher, student to student)

There are, of course, other aspects you might want to use. Feel free to improvise. (Use a separate sheet of paper for your lesson profile.)

After completing a lesson profile, consider asking to see the cooperating teacher's lesson plan, if one exists. Compare the plan with the profile.

What, if any, tentative conclusions do you have regarding this teacher's perspective? For example:

1. How responsive does the teacher appear to be to moods or interests of the learners? To what extent does any discrepancy between the lesson plan and the profile represent the responsiveness of the cooperating teacher?
2. Does the cooperating teacher treat different learners differently in terms of grouping, time allocation, tasks, standards, etc.?
3. How much of the lesson is done by learners individually and how much in groups? Is there a spirit of competition or cooperation in the groups? Does the cooperating teacher say or do anything to encourage or discourage this spirit?
4. How formal/informal does the cooperating teacher appear? What does the cooperating teacher do to develop or reinforce this role?
5. What seems to be the point of the lesson? For example, is it to memorize some material, share some ideas, find some "correct" answers or procedures, check to see if the learners have been doing their work, or to clarify ideas? How does the cooperating teacher communicate the intent to the class?

▶

---

### EXERCISE 9.4   Analysis of Lesson Elements

You can take your observation one step further by applying a template to the lesson, that is, looking for a set of basic elements. For our present purposes we will consider a relatively simple and straightforward approach to the analysis of lessons, adapted from the work of Hunter.[9] Hunter provides an outline of the basic elements of a lesson, which can function as a set of questions to answer as you observe the teacher in action:

1. *Anticipatory set.* What has the teacher done to get the students' attention, to relate the lesson to what the students have done previously, and to engage them in the lesson? Look for how the teacher communicates to students that the lesson is about to begin, whether the teacher reviews previous lessons, how the teacher tries to stimulate interest, and what the teacher does to lay the groundwork for the lesson.

▶

2. *Objective and purpose.* What has the teacher done to communicate to the students what they are supposed to get out of the lesson and why that is important?

▶

3. *Input.* What knowledge and skills necessary to achieve the lesson's objective does the teacher make available to the students, and how does the teacher provide them? Look for the specific methods employed, whether they include lecture, discussion, laboratory, seatwork, or some other method.

▶

4. *Modeling.* How does the teacher show the students what they are expected to produce or learn to do? What kinds of examples and demonstrations are employed?

▶

5. *Checking for understanding.* How does the teacher monitor the students' understanding of concepts and proficiency in skills during the lesson? How does the teacher adjust the lesson on the basis of this feedback? Look for the ways in which the teacher invites questions, how the teacher asks and answers questions (including the amount of time the teacher waits for an answer), how many and what type of students the teacher involves in questioning, and what the teacher does with a student's answer, especially when it is wrong.

▶

6. *Guided practice.* How does the teacher give the students opportunities to practice using their new knowledge or skill under direct teacher supervision?

▶

7. *Independent practice.* How does the teacher provide opportunities for students to practice using their new knowledge or skills independently after the teacher is reasonably sure that students will not make serious errors?

▶

As Hunter points out, a common error in the observation of teaching is the belief that "all good things must be in every lesson."[10] The teacher must decide which of the elements to include, as well as how to include it. The advantage of templates like Hunter's is that they give us things to look for; the disadvantage is that the template is not appropriate for every lesson. Figuring out why particular elements are absent from a lesson can provide important insights into teaching in its own right.

The classroom and the curriculum used by the teacher function as both resources and constraints for your teaching. As resources, they provide a structure within which you can work and a set of ideas, materials, equipment, and spaces that you can utilize for your lessons. As constraints, they limit what you can teach and how you can teach it. Whatever you do in the classroom will have to fit into an existing curricular and classroom framework.

A glass is both half empty and half full, depending on how you want to look at it. Whether you choose to consider the classroom and the curriculum as resources or constraints, it should be clear that you will need to understand how they function. Take the time now to jot down any thoughts you might have about these two important aspects of teaching that you will want to consider as you plan your teaching.

▶

With these thoughts in mind, it is time to consider the most significant factor affecting what and how you teach, namely, the students themselves.

## NOTES

1. Dan Lortie, *Schoolteacher* (Chicago: University of Chicago Press, 1975).
2. Ibid., p. 61.
3. Ibid.
4. Ibid., p. 62.
5. Rob Walker and Clem Adelman, *A Guide to Classroom Observation* (London: Methuen, 1975).
6. Ibid., p. 8.
7. Adapted from ibid.
8. Ibid., p. 25.
9. Madeline Hunter, "Knowing, Teaching and Supervising," in *Using What We Know about Teaching,* ed. Philip Hosford (Alexandria, Va.: Association for Supervision and Curriculum Development, 1984), pp. 169–192.
10. Ibid., p. 176.

# chapter 10

# The Students

**O**ur memories are remarkably short. It was not very long ago that you were students in school. Yet most college students have difficulty seeing school and teachers in the same way school-age children do. And the younger the schoolchildren, the greater the gap between your and their perspectives. Nevertheless, one of the most valuable things that teachers can possess is an understanding of how their students view themselves and the school. With this understanding, we are in a better position to appreciate the way students experience school and how our teaching affects that experience.

Clearly, school is not just the building and the teachers within it; school is also (and, perhaps, more significantly for children) a place to interact with other children. That is, school is also a social experience. Therefore, we are interested not only in the students' backgrounds and interests but also in the ways the students regard one another, the ways they interact within groups, and the ways groups of children interact. In short, we are also interested in learning about the student culture.

## STUDENTS IN THE SCHOOL

By studying the students, you can find out the composition of the student population and what it is like being a student in a particular school. These two aspects of school life are best identified through a combination of talks with and observations of the students. Here are some suggestions.

### EXERCISE 10.1   Conversations with Students in the School

During recesses and lunchtime, or after school, try to talk with at least one student. You might want to tell the student that you are not reporting to anybody, that you just want to find out about the school in which you will be working.

You might ask about the student's neighborhood. Are the people there like the people in the school? How are they different?

What does the student want to do after leaving school? Has he or she made any plans? If the student is old enough, ask if he or she works after school hours or during vacations.

Does the student like school? What about it does he or she like and dislike? What is the student's favorite subject? What about it does he or she like? Ask similar questions about the subject the student dislikes the most and the subject in which the student does the best and the worst. What about extracurricular activities, including sports?

Who is the student's favorite teacher this year? Who is the favorite teacher of all time? Would most others agree? What makes this teacher the best? You might try to identify the characteristics of this student's "ideal" teacher.

Who are the student's friends? Is this student in a clique? If so, what is it like? Who in the school does he or she like or dislike? What does he or she like or dislike about these kids? Whose opinion really counts?

Are there kids in the school who are very "different"? What makes them "different"? How does this student feel about kids who are "different"?

How much help does this student receive from his or her parents? What kind of help? With homework or projects? Moral support? Has this student ever been in trouble in school? What kind? How did the parents react? What does the school do when kids cause trouble?

After talking to a few students, try to summarize your notes here, comparing and contrasting the students' backgrounds, goals and aspirations, likes and dislikes, ideal teacher, friendship groups, attitudes about people who are "different," and the role of their parents in their schooling.

*Backgrounds:*
▶

*Goals and aspirations:*
▶

*Likes and dislikes:*
▶

*Ideal teacher:*
▶


*Friendship groups and "significant others":*
▶


*Attitudes about people who are "different":*
▶


*Parents' role:*
▶


---

**EXERCISE 10.2    Observing Students in the School**

You might also try to observe some students. The cafeteria during lunch and the playground or school grounds during recess are possible places.

*Dress.* How are the children dressed? Comment on neatness and apparent affluence. Also note differences in dress among groups of children.

*Language.* What is their out-of-class language like? How is it different from their in-class language? What sorts of emotions do they express with their language? Do they use abusive language? Note differences in languages among groups of children. Do some groups use language as a code to keep their members separated from other groups?

*Interests.* If you are unobtrusive, you will be able to overhear fragments of conversations. What do the children talk about? Teachers? Sports and cars? Grades? The opposite sex? Clothes? Current events? Tests? Note differences in topics of conversation for different groups. Do some groups talk about other groups?

*Groups.* What groups can you identify? (Groups are particularly noticeable in secondary schools.) Some groups you might notice are "jocks," "druggies," "skaters," "snobs," "nerds," "preppies," and students of various racial or ethnic backgrounds. How would you characterize each group? Consider dress, language, race, interests, how physical, materialistic, and so on. How rigid is group definition? That is, are some students members of more than one group? Or do some members of groups mix with members of other groups? Are there loners? What are their characteristics?

*Territory.* Does each of the groups have its own "territory"? Which one has the most territory? The least territory? How closely guarded is each group's territory?

*Conflict.* What sorts of conflict do you observe? Are the protagonists members of different groups? What is the source of the conflict (e.g., physical or verbal abuse, invasion of one group's territory by another)? How is the conflict settled (if at all) and by whom?

*Dominance and Power.* Do any of the groups appear to be dominant? Which are the most and the least powerful groups? What is the source of each group's power (e.g., academic skills, athletic skill, muscle, "street knowledge")? Do any of the groups depend on adult approval for their power?

Summarize what you have found about the students in the school. Who are they and what is it like to "live" in this school?

▶

## STUDENTS IN THE CLASSROOM

"Every person is unique." Although most teachers would agree with this statement, they tend to talk about student types—slow learners, underachievers, disadvantaged, at risk, science oriented, jocks, or college bound. This tendency is understandable in all people when they try to reduce the complexity of a situation. Typing students transforms a room filled with 35 unique individuals to one with 3, 5, or even 10 types of students. But however understandable or natural this tendency, it is also potentially dangerous, because such a practice might blind teachers to their students' individuality. This is why you should get to know your students as individuals. Each has particular strengths and weaknesses, likes and dislikes, and desirable and undesirable traits. Not only is each student an individual, but each is also a member of one or more friendship groups. Understanding who a student looks to for approval or respect is also of vital importance.

The first step in getting acquainted with the students is to observe them in class. Here is one approach to observing students.

### EXERCISE 10.3   Who Are the Students in the Classroom?[1]

Stand as unobtrusively as possible in the classroom before any students arrive. Jot down notes as they begin to arrive. Some suggestions are as follows:

1. Notice who arrives first and last.
2. How many and of what age and gender are the students in this class?
3. Do students remain in the same groups inside the classroom as those in which they arrived?

4. Look at the overall spacing between groups. Is it uniform? Does it reflect furniture, resource location, or friendship groups? Are there any cliques?

5. Who are the isolates?

6. How much movement between groups occurs? Note how changes in groupings occur during the class period.

7. What roles do particular students play? For example, who is the joker, the cynic, the teacher's pet, the introvert, etc.?

8. Which students raise their hands most often and least often (or never) when the teacher asks a question?

9. On which students does the teacher never call?

10. Is the behavior of the students who sit in the back of the room different from that of the rest of the class? What about the corners, the middle, and the front?

11. Which students seem to be paying the most and the least attention, and what is the range of attention spans?

12. Which students ask for most help and whom do they ask (the teacher, nearby students)?

13. Which students receive the most praise and which receive the most criticism? Which students seem to be ignored?

14. Try to determine the extent of any division of labor in the class or within the groups. Are there different roles? Do all carry out the same tasks? Are roles and tasks fixed, or do they shift among students? Who seems to assign these roles or tasks? How smooth running and cohesive is the class and each group?

15. If there are groups, how much communication and sharing exist among them?

16. Is the relationship among the students mostly cooperative, competitive, or individualistic? For example, when the teacher asks a student a question, do other students help the first student answer it, or do they try to answer it themselves?

17. On which students does the teacher rely to help decide when to move on? When teachers decide to move on to another activity or topic, they commonly base this decision on their judgment that certain students have "gotten" the material. This group of students has been termed the "steering group."[2] Where do these students stand in relation to the rest of the class in terms of ability?

Summarize your observations of the students in the classroom. What are the prominent groups and how do the groups interact? Which individuals play key roles in relationships among students and in terms of the lesson flow?

▶

Are students that belong to a minority group treated differently than others? Do any of these students appear to participate in the classroom to a greater or lesser degree? Are there certain kinds of activities in which minority students are more or less engaged?

▶

## NOTES

1. Rob Walker and Clem Adelman, *A Guide to Classroom Observation* (London: Methuen, 1975).
2. Urban Dahllof, *Ability Grouping, Content Validity and Curriculum Process Analysis* (New York: Teacher's College Press, 1971).

chapter **11**

# The Cooperating Teacher

$\mathbf{P}$robably the greatest influence on the quality of a field experience, particularly for the student teacher, is the cooperating teacher. In a sense, the student teacher is an apprentice and the cooperating teacher is a master teacher. Even in many less formal arrangements, such as exploratory field experiences, there is a cooperating teacher on whom the success of the field experience depends. Cooperating teachers always do some things that the student teacher disagrees with or does not understand. The purpose of this chapter is not to persuade you that the cooperating teacher knows best. Instead, it is meant to help you understand how the cooperating teacher views teaching and to see the situation through his or her eyes.

---

### EXERCISE 11.1   Conversation with the Teacher

If you can arrange one, a get-acquainted meeting with the cooperating teacher could prove informative.

One purpose of a conversation with the cooperating teacher is to find out the teacher's perspective on teaching and the beliefs underlying the teacher's actions. In order to meet this purpose, objectivity and suspension of judgment are important, even if you strongly disagree with what you hear.

There are many questions you might ask the cooperating teacher. I have organized a series of questions into a set of eight issues. Rather than try to cover all eight in the limited time you can reasonably expect the cooperating teacher to give you, you could select the two or three that interest you most. Your interests may derive from the amount of thought you have personally given to the issues or from the apparent significance of the issues to the cooperating teacher based on your classroom observations.

The eight issues are as follows (numbers in parentheses refer to the questions in the list following this one):

1. Control
   a. How are decisions made about teaching methods? (1, 2, 3, 5, 6, 9, 11)
   b. How are decisions made about curriculum and content? (4, 5, 9, 10, 11)
   c. How much and what kind of control should teachers have over pupils' behavior? (7, 8, 18)
2. Diversity
   a. What learner differences are significant, and should different types of learners be treated differently? (12)
3. Learning
   a. Is learning facilitated by a competitive or cooperative environment? (14)
   b. What is the basis of motivation? (14)
4. Teacher's Role
   a. How formal a role should the teacher assume? (13)
5. School and Society
   a. How active should a teacher become in political reform? (15)
   b. Should the school reflect the current society or attempt to reform it? (15)
6. Knowledge
   a. What should be the curriculum's emphasis? (16, 18)
   b. Should subject matters be kept separate or integrated? (17)
7. Rewards and Criteria
   a. What are the rewards of teaching? (19)
   b. What are the criteria by which teachers should be evaluated? (20, 21)
8. CT-ST Relationship
   a. What should be the role of the student teacher? (22, 23)

Try to select a time when the cooperating teacher is alone in the classroom or somewhere outside when distractions are minimal. Here are some suggestions for questions covering the eight issues. You will probably have to modify them in your own meeting. Some of the questions might best be left until a future meeting after you have established a better relationship with the cooperating teacher.

1. I've noticed some special areas in your room. (Specify one of them.) What do you and the kids do in this area? Who gets to use it? How are they selected? (Repeat for each area.)
2. Did you arrange the room this way ? (If no): Who did? (If yes): What were you trying to do with this arrangement? How long has it been this way?
3. Did you put up the posters, pictures, exhibits, etc., on the walls and bulletin boards? (If no): Who did? (If yes): What was the purpose? When did you put them up? (May be different for each poster.)
4. I've been looking through the textbook. How was it selected and by whom? How do you like it? What are its strengths? Weaknesses? Is it successful with some kids but not with others? (Repeat this set of questions for each text.)
5. I also looked over the worksheets, labs, and/or quizzes you've been using. Did you write them? (If no): Where did you get them? (If yes): When did you make them up? Did you base them on anything in particular? Are you happy with them?
6. I enjoyed the lesson(s) (or classes) that I had the opportunity to observe. When I compared your lesson plan with the actual lesson, I noticed that you did not follow

your plan precisely. (This question is used only if you noticed some discrepancies.) What caused you to modify your plan?

7. What rules do you expect the kids in your class to follow? (*Probe:* rules for waiting their turn to speak and to receive help, rules for moving around the classroom, leaving the classroom, being on time, what to do when finished with work, working together, resolving conflicts among kids, homework, forms to follow, procedures for work, language, noises, who may speak, etc.) Does the school have rules or regulations with which you disagree? (If yes): Why do you disagree? Do you follow them anyway? Which rules are the most important to you? How do you handle infractions? Are there some kids who break rules more than other kids? Tell me about those kids.

8. How do you enforce your rules? What happens when someone breaks one? Does it depend on who that kid is? Do you ever feel you are losing control of the class? How do you go about regaining control?

9. Do parents ever visit the classroom? (If no): Would you like them to? (If yes): Are you pleased that they do? How can parents be of most help to you as a teacher? How can they hinder you? Should parents be involved in selection of school books? What about in hiring teachers?

10. Does the school or the district have a curriculum? Are you expected to follow it? Do you? Did you have any say in it? Do you ever depart from it?

11. Do your students' (or "children's," for primary grades) interests affect your teaching methods? (If yes): In what ways? Do their interests affect the content? Do they have any say in what they study? (If yes): In what ways?

12. What sorts of students do you teach? Are there different groups? Could you describe the groups? Do you devote more time to certain students? Do you expect all of them to assume the same degree of responsibility for their learning? Do you use different criteria to evaluate different students? Do you find the diversity among them to be a major problem?

13. How friendly are you with the children? Do you tell them much about yourself? What do you think is the proper role for a teacher?

14. Do you try to develop a sense of competition in your class? How important is cooperating among the kids? What do you use to motivate the kids? (*Probe:* grades, interest and curiosity, comparison of one child's work with another's, fear.)

15. Do you ever let the kids know your political views? Do you think that the schools are doing a pretty good job or do they need to change drastically? Are you trying to help kids fit into the society as it is, or would you like to equip them to reform society?

16. How important are the three Rs to you? What about the children's emotional needs? Are they important? What about things like problem-solving skills and creativity—are they important? What is the relative importance of these various goals?

17. Do you ever try to relate one subject matter (e.g., science) with another that you or another teacher teaches? Or do you think different subject matters should be treated separately?

18. What do you test for? How important are your tests and quizzes?

19. Most people have days in their work when they go home feeling especially good because the day and its activities were particularly rewarding. What makes a good day in teaching for you?

20. How do you tell how well you are doing as a teacher? That is, what things provide you with evidence that you're doing a good job?

21. Suppose you accidentally happened to overhear a group of your former students discussing you as a teacher. What kinds of things would you like to hear them saying?

22. Why did you ask to have a student teacher (or aide, depending on your role)?

23. What do you expect from me?

On the following Teacher Analysis Form, you can summarize the cooperating teacher's responses in column 3 for each issue (expressed as a general question in column 1). The number of the question sets that correspond to the issue are listed in column 2.

### FORM 11.1   Teacher Analysis Form

| (1)<br>Issue | (2)<br>Question Set Number | (3) |
|---|---|---|
| **1.** *Control*<br>    **a.** How are decisions made about teaching? | **1.** Special areas<br>**2.** Room arrangement<br>**3.** Posters, pictures, etc.<br>**5.** Worksheets/labs/quizzes<br>**6.** Modification of lesson plan<br>**9.** Parents visiting classrooms<br>**11.** Student interest affecting teaching methods | |
|     **b.** How are decisions made about curriculum and content? | **4.** Textbook(s)<br>**5.** Worksheets/labs/quizzes<br>**9.** Parents visiting classrooms<br>**10.** School curriculum<br>**11.** Student interest affecting teaching methods | |
|     **c.** How much and what kind of control should teachers have over pupils' behavior? | **7.** Rules/regulations<br>**8.** Enforcement of rules<br>**18.** Tests | |
| **2.** *Diversity*<br>    **a.** What pupil differences are significant and should different pupils be treated differently? | **12.** Groups of children and their treatment | |
| **3.** *Learning*<br>    **a.** Is learning facilitated by a competitive or cooperative environment? | **14.** Competition/cooperation/ motivation of students | |
|     **b.** What is the basis for motivation? | **14.** Competition/cooperation/ motivation of students | |

4. *Teacher's Role*
   a. How formal a role should the teacher assume in the classroom?

5. *School and Society*
   a. How active should the teacher become in political reform?
   b. Should the school reflect the current society or attempt to reform it?

6. *Knowledge*
   a. What should be the curriculum's emphasis?
   b. Should subject matters be kept separate or integrated?

7. *Rewards and Criteria*
   a. What are the rewards of teaching?
   b. What are the criteria by which teachers should be evaluated?

8. *CT-ST Relationship*
   a. What should be the role of the student teacher?

13. Teacher's personal relationship with students

15. Political views and reform

15. Political views and reform

16. Three Rs emotional needs, etc.
18. Areas tested
17. Separate subject matters

19. Good days

20. Doing a good job
21. Overhearing students

22. Reason for having an ST
23. Expectations

---

This information about your cooperating teacher is useful for two principal reasons. It prepares you for work within this teacher's classroom and with this teacher's students, and it helps you decide the kind of relationship you may want to develop with this teacher.

First, because the CT sets the scene for your field experience, the more you know about the CT's perspective on teaching, the more you will understand the context of your own teaching. The CT develops in students a set of expectations for "normal" classroom activities and standards of appropriate classroom behaviors and acceptable student performance. These expectations affect how the students will react to any activities in which you try to engage them. For example, if the teacher normally has the students work individually on worksheets at their desks, you might experience some difficulty in having students work cooperatively in small groups on projects.

Second, the degree of comfort you feel with the CT's perspective might help you determine the kind of relationship you want to develop with the CT. At one extreme, if the CT represents all you want to become as a teacher, then you might want to serve in the role of an apprentice for this master teacher. If, on the other extreme, the CT represents the opposite of what you wish to become as a teacher, then you might try to establish as much autonomy as possible during the field experience, perhaps working independently with a small group of students on a separate project. Clearly, you are not the only one who determines your role. Both the CT and your college supervisor contribute to the definition of what counts as an appropriate role. However, it will be useful at least to understand the situation that your feelings toward the CT create for your field experience.

part **IV**

# What Have You Learned?

# chapter 12

# The Progress Report

An experience is educational, if we learn something from it. If your field experience is to be educational, then it will have to help you learn something about teaching, about yourself, about learners, about your subject matter, or about the social milieu in which teaching occurs. This chapter is intended to help you crystallize some of the things you learned from your field experience thus far.

Your field experience has likely reinforced certain prior beliefs and challenged others, introduced you to new ways of thinking about some familiar things, and helped you find out more about teaching and your future in it. Now might be a good time to try to make that learning explicit.

Taking stock of learning (or anything else) is best done on paper. A progress report, whether written in the middle or at the end of a field experience, is one useful device for this purpose. Here you will find one approach to progress reports focusing on what you learned about teaching and, more specifically, on your perspective on teaching. Although I will suggest a particular format for this report, you or your college supervisor may prefer a different format. Obviously, you should follow whatever format is most appropriate to your own situation.

If you look for models to follow when writing your report, you will probably be surprised. Few books exist that provide a bridge between theory and practice. There are many books that present abstract ideas about what or how to teach and characteristics of a "good" teacher, drawing on educational psychology, sociology, and philosophy as well as teaching experience. Also there are many books that offer purely anecdotal information about teaching.[1] However, few books exist that present principles, ideals, or issues about teaching, together with anecdotes for illustrative purposes.[2] Even fewer are written by teachers and present integrated perspectives on teaching together with anecdotal information.[3] Some of this sort do exist in fields other than teaching, such as in psychotherapy.[4]

In order to give you a clear idea of what a progress report might look like and how it serves as a bridge between theory and practice, I will suggest one possible format for a progress report. In addition, Appendix B presents some students' actual progress reports.

## THE ANATOMY OF A PROGRESS REPORT

One format for progress reports that has proven useful contains the following questions:

1. What was (or is) the context of your field experience?
2. What were your goals for the field experience?
3. What did you learn about teaching in that situation (in terms of principles, ideals, or issues)?
4. What happened (in terms of episodes) during your field experience to cause you to learn those things?
5. How generalizable to other teaching situations are the things you learned?
6. How successful were you in achieving your goals?

### Context

Introduce your progress report with two or three paragraphs about the situation in which your field experience is taking place. To do this, refer back to the situation analysis you wrote earlier (Chapters 8 through 11). As you did then, describe the school and community, then the classroom, the curriculum, and the cooperating teacher. Try to write this section as background material for the reader. That is, set the stage for the drama that you will unfold.

### Goals

Given this situation, what were your goals? Describe briefly the goals you set for yourself (refer to Chapter 2) and for the learners (refer to Chapter 7). This section is not just a restatement of work you did in previous chapters. During your field experience, your goals likely shifted as you realized more realistically what could and should be accomplished. Therefore, try to describe any modifications in goals and reasons for the changes, because, in part, the changes reflect your growth from the experience.

### Learning

The heart of the report and of your field experience itself is what you learned from the experience. Both your goals for yourself and your learning may have been multi-faceted. For the purpose of this report, focus on what you learned about teaching. Although this focus limits the scope of the section on learning, there is still much room for diversity. What you learned about teaching might represent answers to one or more of the following questions:

1. What are the characteristics of an effective (successful or good) teacher? Answers to this question take the following form:
    Effective teachers are _____ (e.g., enthusiastic about their subject matter, caring, flexible, etc.).
2. What are the characteristics of an effective (successful, worthwhile, or good) lesson? Answer:
    A lesson is effective if _____ (e.g., children are actively involved).
3. What are crucial (or important) teaching skills? Answer:
    _____ (e.g., probing questions) is a crucial teaching skill.
4. What should teachers attempt to do or accomplish? Answer:
    Teachers should attempt to _____ (e.g., build self-confidence, set a good example, enter students' frame of reference, establish good rapport, emphasize the positive, gain respect of students, etc.).
5. What are important dilemmas that teachers face? Answer:
    An important dilemma that teachers face is _____ (e.g., whether to establish an informal or more formal teacher role; how to modify and direct teaching toward each student's need with 30 students in each class).

Questions 1, 2, and 4 address ideals of teaching. Question 3 obviously focuses on skills. Question 5 reflects unresolved issues that surface as a result of encountering problems.

Question 5 is the most open-ended, recognizing that field experience raises more issues than it resolves. This question draws directly on Chapters 4 through 7. Questions 1 and 4 draw directly on Chapter 6.

These five questions do not exhaust the conclusions you might reach regarding teaching. Others include the needs of children (e.g., the need to be recognized), how children learn (e.g., learning is an active process), things of which teachers should be aware (e.g., different comprehension skills of children), and problems children face (e.g., identity crises). Whatever you did learn about teaching, make it explicit in your report.

## Episodes

Presumably, what you learned about teaching you learned from some episodes that occurred during your field experience. Typically, these episodes represent either successes or failures that taught you something important. It is this aspect of your report that most heavily depends on your weekly logs (see Chapter 3). Logs provide case material, and this case material serves as illustrations of issues and evidence for conclusions you described in the preceding section on ideals, skills, and dilemmas of teaching.

The two sections on "learning" and "episodes" are best treated as one integrated section. To interweave the two, you might proceed as follows:

1. Succinctly propose an ideal, skill, or dilemma of teaching. An example dilemma would be how much emphasis to place on real understanding or mastery of content while still covering all required topics.
2. Develop an argument for the importance of that particular ideal, skill, or dilemma; for example, every time a teacher decides whether to entertain more student questions or terminate discussion of a topic, how quickly to pace a lecture, or how much emphasis to place on individual student project work, the teacher confronts the depth (i.e., mastery) versus breadth (i.e., coverage) dilemma.
3. Describe in detail from your logs one or two episodes that occurred that made you realize the importance of that particular ideal, skill, or dilemma.
4. Repeat 1, 2, and 3.

My students have found that anywhere between three and seven proposition-argument–episode items provide sufficient food for thought.

## Generalizability

Your report centers on what you learned from a *specific* situation, thus a brief discussion is helpful to address the generalizability of your conclusions. Would the same ideals, skills, or dilemmas apply to larger or smaller groups; to other subject matters; to different age students (and teachers); to students with special problems; and to other institutional, administrative, or societal contexts? This section, like the previous one, might be interwoven with the section on learnings, thus forming a set of learning-argument–episode–generalizability statements.

## Goal Achievement

Reflecting back on your goals (see Chapters 2 and 7), try to assess the success you had in achieving those goals during your field experience.

If, like most people, you did not accomplish all you intended, consider the reasons for lack of goal achievement:

1. Unrealistic goals (e.g., not enough time)
2. Outside influences beyond your control (e.g., student's family)
3. Limitations in your own motivation or perseverance
4. Specific knowledge or skills you lacked
5. Specific traits you lacked
6. Your cooperating teacher
7. Your college supervisor
8. The principal

The sample progress reports written by students (see Appendix B) will not only give you an idea of what a progress report looks like, but also inspire you to make the most of this opportunity to reflect on your field experience. The format options presented here are intended to increase the depth of this reflection.

## EPILOGUE

When I was a student in school, I could never understand why people called the end point of schooling "commencement." It was so confusing to me that I found myself using the word "commence" to mean "terminate." Of course, commencement referred to the beginning of life after school. What I realized much later is that we can consider the conclusion of any experience as a commencement, a period of getting ready for the next experience.

This book has focused on preparing for and reflecting on one particular experience. The conclusion of one particular experience is an opportune time for both reflection and preparation. It is a time to think back over one teaching experience and attempt to use it as a basis for planning the next experience.

Now might be a good time to make some plans for the future. While your field experience is still fresh in your mind, consider the following questions:

**1. a.** What issues have been raised by your field experience? Which ones remain unresolved?

▶

    **b.** What sorts of experiences do you think will enable you to work out some of these issues?

▶

**2. a.** What teaching skills do you need to work on?

▶

    **b.** How might you work on them?

▶

**3.** What kinds of teaching situations do you now need to try?

▶

4. What should you be doing in the meantime (e.g., types of books to read, people to talk with, observations to make)?

▶

## NOTES

1. Kevin Ryan, *The Roller Coaster Year* (New York: HarperCollins, 1992).
2. Raymond Corsini and Daniel Howard, *Critical Incidents in Teaching* (Englewood Cliffs, N.J.: Prentice-Hall, 1964).
3. Eliot Wigginton, *Sometimes a Shining Moment* (New York: Doubleday Books, 1985); Nancy Wallace, *Better Than School* (Burdett, N.Y.: Larson, 1983); Sylvia Ashton-Warner, *Teacher* (New York: Bantam Books, 1963); A. S. Neill, *Summerhill: A Radical Approach to Child Rearing* (New York: Hart, 1960).
4. Virginia Axline, *Dibs: In Search of Self* (Boston: Houghton Mifflin, 1964).

# Appendixes

Appendixes

# Instruments

## THE STUDENT BELIEF INVENTORY

Many of the beliefs we hold as teachers are derived from our perspectives as students. Later in this appendix you will respond to a set of statements designed to help you identify your perspective on your field experience as a teacher. In this exercise you will respond to a set of statements intended to elicit your perspective on being a student.

Note: 1    Strongly disagree ("For the most part, no")

       2    Disagree but with major qualifications ("No, but . . .")

       3    Agree but with major qualifications ("Yes, but . . .")

       4    Strongly agree ("For the most part, yes")

### *Control*

**1.** My instructors should have complete control over each of the following:

1 2 3 4    a. teaching methods

1 2 3 4    b. classroom rules

1 2 3 4    c. selection of textbooks

1 2 3 4    d. curriculum and goals

1 2 3 4    e. administration of the school

**2.** Each of the following individuals or groups should have a say in educational decisions that affect each of my classes:

1 2 3 4    a. college administrators

1 2 3 4    b. the faculty member in charge

1 2 3 4        c. other faculty members
1 2 3 4        d. myself
1 2 3 4        e. my parents
1 2 3 4        f. state officials
1 2 3 4        g. students in each class

**3.** Each of the following individuals or groups should have a say in the courses I take:

1 2 3 4        a. faculty members
1 2 3 4        b. state officials
1 2 3 4        c. my parents
1 2 3 4        d. myself
1 2 3 4        e. college administrators

## Diversity

**4.** As a student I want to be treated like all other students when it comes to each of the following:

1 2 3 4        a. methods
1 2 3 4        b. evaluation criteria
1 2 3 4        c. time offered to students
1 2 3 4        d. teacher's expectations for my achievement level

## Learning

1 2 3 4   **5.** I learn best when lessons are laid out as a series of carefully sequenced steps.

1 2 3 4   **6.** I learn best when left on my own to figure things out.

1 2 3 4   **7.** My motivation for learning derives more from intrinsic interest and curiosity than from external rewards.

## Role of the Teacher

1 2 3 4   **8.** It is more important for me to respect than to like my instructors.

1 2 3 4   **9.** I prefer my instructors to be friendly and personal rather than to project a businesslike attitude.

## School and Society

1 2 3 4   **10.** I don't think it proper for my instructors to let students know about their political preferences or their criticisms of the college administration.

1 2 3 4   **11.** Everything that I learn is related to every other thing.

1 2 3 4   **12.** All students (including myself) should have to study a core of studies that represent the basic elements of a good education.

1 2 3 4   **13.** My education should emphasize a broad background in the liberal arts, rather than specialized training.

It might be interesting to compare your responses on this Student Belief Inventory with those of your classmates. How do you account for differences and similarities? Another interesting comparison is your responses to the Student Belief Inventory versus your responses to the Teacher Belief Inventory that follows. While responding to the statements in the Teacher Belief Inventory, you will be able to reflect on the degree to which your perspective on teaching has been influenced by your student perspective and the appropriateness of one to the other.

## THE TEACHER BELIEF INVENTORY[1]

What if in your field experience you were fully responsible for the learners? Would you be the same teacher as the cooperating teacher or your co-worker(s) (if any), or would you differ in significant ways?

This exercise is designed to help you sort out your beliefs. In order to do it, you must decide the extent to which you, as the teacher in charge, agree or disagree with each of the following assertions. If you are not actually the teacher in charge in your field experience, respond *as if you were in charge*. Circle one response for each assertion. Respond only to those assertions that apply to your field experience. You will note that the assertions are grouped under headings corresponding to the six basic issues presented in Chapter 5.

Note: 1   Strongly disagree ("For the most part, no")

2   Disagree but with major qualifications ("No, but . . .")

3   Agree but with major qualifications ("Yes, but . . .")

4   Strongly agree ("For the most part, yes")

### *Control*

1 2 3 4   **1.** I would encourage parents to work with me inside the classroom.

1 2 3 4   **2.** Parents would have no right to tell me as a teacher what to do in the classroom.

1 2 3 4   **3.** As a teacher I should be left free to determine the methods of instruction that I use in the classrooms.

1 2 3 4   **4.** Parents would have the right to visit my classroom at any time if they gave me prior notice.

1 2 3 4   **5.** I would consider the revision of my teaching methods if these were criticized by the learners.

1 2 3 4   **6.** As a teacher I would rely heavily on the textbook and prepackaged materials, rather than trying to write and design my own.

1 2 3 4   **7.** Learners should have some control over the order in which they complete classroom assignments.

1 2 3 4   **8.** Learners should have some choice in the selection of classroom assignments.

1 2 3 4     **9.** I would feel free to depart from the official adopted curriculum when it seemed appropriate to do so.

1 2 3 4     **10.** Parents and other community members should have the right to reject school books and materials.

1 2 3 4     **11.** The principal or my department chairperson should ultimately determine what and how I should teach.

1 2 3 4     **12.** What I teach will probably be heavily influenced by statewide or districtwide standardized tests.

1 2 3 4     **13.** As a teacher my primary task would be to carry out the educational goals and curricular decisions that have been formulated by others.

1 2 3 4     **14.** I would give learners some options for deciding *what* to study.

1 2 3 4     **15.** Parents should be active in formulating the curriculum.

1 2 3 4     **16.** Parents should be involved in hiring teachers for their children's school.

1 2 3 4     **17.** I would be involved in administrative decisions in my school or organization (e.g., allocating the school's budget, hiring staff).

1 2 3 4     **18.** I would disobey official regulations when I felt that they interfered with the welfare of the learners.

1 2 3 4     **19.** I would allow learners to go to the bathroom at just about any time.

1 2 3 4     **20.** It is more important for learners to learn to obey rules than to make their own decisions.

1 2 3 4     **21.** I would encourage learners to speak spontaneously without necessarily raising their hands.

### Diversity

1 2 3 4     **22.** I would employ multiple and diverse criteria to evaluate learners. It is not fair to use the same criteria to evaluate all learners.

1 2 3 4     **23.** If I taught classes that differed with regard to learners' academic ability, I would teach them differently.

1 2 3 4     **24.** I would not expect learners from economically disadvantaged backgrounds to assume the same degree of responsibility for their learning as learners from more economically advantaged backgrounds.

1 2 3 4     **25.** One of the main problems in classrooms today is diversity among pupils.

1 2 3 4     **26.** There should be set standards for each grade level and subject, and as a teacher I would evaluate all learners according to these standards.

1 2 3 4     **27.** I could probably do most for learners who want to learn.

1 2 3 4     **28.** I would attempt to devote more of my time to the least capable learners in order to provide an equal education for all.

1 2 3 4     **29.** I would lower my expectations regarding academic performance for those learners who come from economically disadvantaged backgrounds.

## Learning

1 2 3 4    **30.** One of the most important tasks I would face as a teacher is developing individuals into a good working group.

1 2 3 4    **31.** I would use the comparison of one learner's work with that of another as a method of motivation.

1 2 3 4    **32.** People learn better when cooperating than when competing with one another.

1 2 3 4    **33.** I would lead learners through a series of easily mastered steps in such a way that the learners make as few errors as possible.

1 2 3 4    **34.** I would tell my students exactly what was expected of them in terms of behavior, homework, and lesson objectives.

1 2 3 4    **35.** Because people learn a great deal from their mistakes, I would allow learners to learn by trial and error.

1 2 3 4    **36.** I would use grades to motivate learning.

1 2 3 4    **37.** The sheer interest in learning something new and challenging or of successfully accomplishing a task usually supplies sufficient motivation for learning.

## Teacher's Role

1 2 3 4    **38.** I would start out as a strict disciplinarian and gradually become more approachable as the learners come to respect my authority.

1 2 3 4    **39.** As a teacher I would tell learners a great deal about myself.

1 2 3 4    **40.** I would serve more as a group facilitator than as a transmitter of information.

## School and Society

1 2 3 4    **41.** My political beliefs have no place in my teaching.

1 2 3 4    **42.** Schools and youth groups should seek to help all learners to fit as smoothly as possible into our present society.

1 2 3 4    **43.** I would not participate in local political activities when it involved criticism of local school authorities.

1 2 3 4    **44.** As a teacher I would be concerned with changing society.

1 2 3 4    **45.** There is a great deal that is wrong with the public schools today, and one of my priorities as a teacher would be to contribute as much as possible to the reform of public schooling.

1 2 3 4    **46.** The home backgrounds of many learners are the major reasons that those children do not succeed in school.

1 2 3 4    **47.** Schooling as it now exists helps perpetuate social and economic inequalities in our society.

### *Knowledge*

1 2 3 4   **48.** It is as important for learners to enjoy learning as it is for them to acquire specific skills.

1 2 3 4   **49.** In the elementary grades, instruction in the three Rs should take up most of the school day. Other subject areas (e.g., science, social studies) should be given less emphasis in the curriculum.

1 2 3 4   **50.** Students in high school don't spend enough time on the "basic" subjects.

1 2 3 4   **51.** Most high school courses try to cover too much material, thereby sacrificing real understanding.

1 2 3 4   **52.** My subject matter is more a body of content than it is a set of skills to be mastered.

1 2 3 4   **53.** One of the primary purposes of teaching my subject matter is to develop good work and study habits.

1 2 3 4   **54.** Schools today pay too much attention to the social-emotional needs of children, and not enough emphasis is given to academic skill development.

1 2 3 4   **55.** I would emphasize teaching the three Rs more than the skills of problem solving.

1 2 3 4   **56.** It would be important to me to divide the school day into clearly designated times for different subject areas.

1 2 3 4   **57.** I would teach the knowledge of different subject areas separately, because important knowledge is overlooked when subjects are integrated.

## NOTE

1. This inventory was adapted from an instrument developed by Zeichner and Tabachnick at the University of Wisconsin-Madison.

# Sample Logs and Progress Reports

**SAMPLE LOGS**

## Log for March 15

Time spent: 2:30–4:45 P.M.

### *Sequence of Events*

- I arrived at Explorations and sat down at a table with a few of the students.
- A few minutes later, one student informed me I was in "his" seat.
- We resolved our conflict over the seat and then he started speaking to me.
- One of the supervisors reminded him that he had a lot of work he needed to get done.
- The student reacted by starting an argument with the supervisor and was basically somewhat abusive.
- The supervisor suggested maybe I help him with his letter that he needed to type out.
- The student and I worked on his assignment together.

***Episodes.*** I came in at Explorations at around 2:30 P.M. There were only a few students there and two or three were seated at a table in the center of the room. I sat down with them, said hello, and then listed to some of their conversation. About 5 minutes later, a boy came over. The student was white. He was holding a Walkman that was playing loud enough so that I could hear it was rap. I looked up at the boy for a moment and saw he was staring at me.

"Yo," he said. "You're in my seat."

"This is *your* seat?" I asked. He nodded.

"Do you think I could sit in it for a while?" He stared at me for about 10 or 15 seconds and then nodded again. Then, he began asking me questions: How old was I? Where did I go to school? What was my name? I learned his name was Steve and he was 15. Conversation with Steve ended. He started looking at the group at the table. Though there were empty chairs around, Steve remained standing. The group at the table was in a circle and Steve was standing almost behind them. They were talking about Andrew Dice Clay. Steve laughed along with them. A few times, he started to say, "Did ya ever see the one where . . ." Then someone louder from the group would cut him off. Steve didn't finish his sentence. He then turned to me and said, "Did ya ever see the one where he—(something)." I can't remember what he described because I had never seen Clay perform. I responded that I hadn't. I asked Steve if he liked Clay and then what other comedians he liked. I asked him about the music on his Walkman. (It was Snoop Doggy Dogg.) He offered to let me listen to it.

A few minutes later, most of the other students at the table left for a field trip. Steve decided to stay at Explorations. A supervisor came by and reminded Steve of some things he needed to do. "Steve, remember you have to do both those thank-you letters today. No fooling around like last time." He responded: "My ass! I already did one, okay!?" The supervisor asked Steve "to relax." Steve yelled at her: "Yeah, whatever . . . don't tell me what to do!" Steve made the music higher in his Walkman and put his earphones on. The supervisor didn't leave. After about a minute, Steve took the earphones off. The supervisor said, "I bet Nancy will help you if you ask her." Steve looked at me. I remained silent. "Will ya do my stupid letter with me?" he asked. I nodded.

Steve and I went into the computer room. The computer room is fairly noisy with about half-a-dozen computers. Steve brought up (on the computer) the letter he had already drafted. He had a spelling mistake in almost every word. We went through each word. During the session, Steve continually played with his Walkman. He was trying to find a song he said I'd like. I asked him a few times to wait until we were done with the letter. Also during our session, another girl came by and started playing with Steve's hat. He got up out of his seat, drew back his arm, and yelled: "Touch me again and I'll pound you. Want me to break your arm?" I asked Steve to sit down and then quietly told him I couldn't work with him unless he stopped yelling. I waited a couple of minutes and then he turned his attention back to the computer screen.

For the rest of the session, Steve and I continued in our corrections of the letter. Instead of just giving him the correct spelling, I first asked him to read exactly what he'd written and see if it sounded right. For example, when Steve read "helpfule" he realized the *e* made it sound like "help*fuel*," which was wrong. The other words were very common words that I knew he'd find in any book or newspaper, so I asked Steve to get one of his books and try to find some of these words. Steve found a few and was then able to correct those mistakes himself. Other words I ended up just telling him how to correct. Finally, I asked him to read the entire letter out loud. I told Steve I was impressed with how professional the letter sounded. I asked him if he was happy with the work. He said to me: "Yeah . . . now I can tell her (referring to the supervisor) I *know* the letter's all right. She can't say nothing."

Before I left I asked Steve about listening to his song on his Walkman. He found it for me and I listened to it.

*Analysis.*   These episodes with Steve were significant for me because I felt I made some headway with someone who didn't seem to relate well with others. In the situation where Steve told me to get out of his seat, at first I felt really annoyed. Was I going to allow this 15-year-old to tell me what to do? In looking back, I'm glad I used the approach I used—*not* to assert myself yet with Steve. From his contacts with the supervisor, it seemed Steve probably gets a lot of instruction from people and probably wouldn't have reacted well to my telling him that because I was the "tutor" and he the "student" he'd better not tell me what to do.

When I watched Steve try to interact with his peers I think I saw a different side of him than this "problem child." I saw someone who was really trying to make friends, but who simply couldn't get himself heard. Rather than the loud and abusive side of him I saw later, he seemed to be almost shy. He tried to say things, but when others who seemed to control the conversation more would speak, they would stop him from making himself heard. I think it made Steve feel good to have me talk to him and actually have someone question about him. I especially felt this when Steve offered to let me listen to his Walkman, which he talked so much about.

On my last log it was mentioned that misbehavior could be a sign of low self-esteem in a child. I think for Steve this is applicable. From my observations of Steve with the supervisor, he usually has negative interactions with the supervisors and most of them involve a supervisor telling him what he still has to do, that there shouldn't be fooling around, etc. From Steve's comment after the letter was done, I got the idea that he might often be told he doesn't do something the "right" way. In addition to his poor contacts with adults, he was somewhat isolated from those in his age group. He couldn't successfully involve himself in their conversation. Also, he chose not to go on the field trip, which made me think that perhaps he doesn't usually get too much attention from this group.

I thought it was an effective move for the supervisor to ask Steve to ask me to work with him. By Steve asking me to help him, we kind of established this "working relationship." We weren't just put together like I had been with the other two girls in my last log. At least here, Steve and I did have some sort of a relationship before we began working, so we were both more comfortable and relaxed.

Steve did like having me as a friend, so he was trying to continue that relationship while we worked—for example, by trying to locate the song on his Walkman that he thought I would like. I felt this situation was somewhat sensitive because I wanted to encourage Steve in this more positive interaction with someone, and yet I knew the supervisor would expect something from Steve at the end of the afternoon. Also, I felt I needed to establish with Steve that I could be his friend, but that I was also there to help him with his work. The first time I tried to establish this was by telling Steve that I wanted to listen to his tape—but it would be better if we did that after we were done with our work. Another occasion when my "position" as tutor was important was when Steve got involved in an argument with the girl who was bothering him. After Steve sat down (for the purpose of not having others hear), I quietly told him I couldn't work with him unless he stopped arguing. I was glad that on my second visit to Explorations I was able to assert myself a bit more with a student. I think I felt a little safer taking that step with Steve because we had been talking together for nearly an hour. I think by this time I had done enough things that Steve liked, so he didn't explode at me when I explained how I felt.

In relation to the methods I used for editing Steve's letter, I felt that if I simply gave Steve the correct spelling of the words in this letter, I'd probably lose his attention. This is why I decided to keep Steve busy—for example, having him read the letter, look up words in his books, etc. Also, I noticed Steve would jump in and try to correct a word when I told him it was wrong. He also liked to have control of the "mouse." I felt that by allowing him to look up the words himself, he might get more satisfaction and be more involved in the editing.

I felt it was important to keep my promise of listening to Steve's tape before I left. He seemed proud of his Walkman and enjoyed telling me about the songs on it. Also, this kind of reestablished our personal relationship before I left.

From this fieldwork, I learned about building some sort of relationship with a student so that you have "credits" already stored up. I feel this is something I lacked in my last experience at Explorations, and it made a difference. Also, I learned to control my own natural feelings of frustration (as we talked about in class) in order to be more sensitive to a child. For example, I was on the verge of telling Steve exactly how I felt when he told me I was in his seat, but I decided to use a different strategy.

There is one other interesting note about this fieldwork: I later found out that Steve was usually a serious problem child. He had a long record at Explorations of being hyper and angry. In contrast to my last fieldwork, I discovered this after working with Steve. Although there are some benefits to knowing ahead of time about a child, in our case I'm glad I didn't know these details. If I had, I probably would have been too scared to assert myself at all.

There were some unanswered questions and issues left for me from my fieldwork. For example, I was very unhappy with Steve being so physically threatening to the girl in the computer room. I also felt uncomfortable with the way he spoke to the supervisor. I wanted to explain to him that this was not the appropriate way to deal with someone, but I still felt like that would be somewhat too authoritarian of me at that point. In this area, I concluded that I'd wait until another session with Steve (so I could develop even more of a relationship with him) before I try to discuss with him these reactions.

Overall, I was pleased with the session and the fact that we were able to combine doing our work with developing a positive relationship. In addition, the supervisor later said to me: "We haven't seen Steve sit quietly for that long in quite a while." That did make me feel good and also made me want to make even more progress with Steve. Hopefully, I'll get the chance to work with him again.

## Log for May 2

Time spent: 12:30–2:30 P.M.

*Sequence of Events*

- 12:30–1:05 tutored Robbie (social studies)
- 1:10–2:00 tutored Mitch (social studies)

*Episodes.*    Robbie was given a packet of Civil War worksheets in social studies today. Throughout the packet are assignments that are worth points. He can do any of the activities in the packet that he chooses to do, and the packet is due on June 3. Grades are assigned according to how many points you get. For example, an A is about 400–460 points. Therefore, the student could choose to get a C by only doing activities that will add up to the number of points needed for a C. One activity is to define words in terms of the Civil War. Each definition is worth 1 point. Another assignment is to write a newspaper article describing a certain Civil War battle. This would be worth 10 points, 20 points if accompanied by a drawing. Robbie and I were working outside the tutoring room for about 5 minutes before he asked if we could go to the library to use the reference books. He had decided to work on a 20-point table of the major battles of the Civil War. He looked under battles in the encyclopedia and asked if he should be looking up each specific battle instead. I told him that would probably work and he came back with two of the C encyclopedias. We looked up one battle and it said to look under Civil War for a table of the major battles. This table had all the battles he needed to find, so he began filling out his table.

As he was working, he showed me the grading scale and said that he really wanted to work hard on this packet because he thought that he had enough time so that he would be able to get an A. He said that he very much wanted to get an A on this assignment. Before Robbie had gotten to the office, the guidance counselor showed me the report card he got last week for the last grading period. He had gone up in every subject by at least part of a grade (C  to B  ), and he had gone from a D  to a B  in social studies. Social studies is the subject that we have worked on the most. Robbie only had trouble filling out one portion of the chart. The last section asked which side won each battle. The chart in the encyclopedia did not simply say that either the North or the South won. Instead, the book might say that the Confederates were forced to retreat. Robbie didn't know if *Confederate* meant North or South, so I had him look it up in the dictionary. There were also a few ambiguous terms that he did not understand, so I would have him read another part of the encyclopedia to find the answer. Even when he didn't know a term, Robbie would read the description to me and ask if that meant that a certain side won. When he used this technique, he only guessed wrong once. He was even able to give reasons why he thought that an unfamiliar term meant that a certain side won. Robbie and I filled in about half of his table by the time he had to leave.

I met Mitch's social studies teacher today. Mitch was late and I asked if she knew where he might be. She asked who I was and told me that she was his teacher and that he needed to study for a unit test. She explained that he couldn't remember what he read the week before, so I said I would help him study for the test. When I found Mitch he said that he didn't know he had a test. I checked again and the test she was talking about is next week. Therefore, I asked if he had anything else to work on. Before he could answer, his teacher came in the room and questioned him for about 10 minutes on whether he had done this or that assignment. When she left, Mitch said that he had not done any of the things he had told her he'd done and wasn't going to because she was mean. We talked about this for a few minutes, and his teacher came back again. This time she told me that he was not supposed to know which questions to do, because she wanted him to read the chapter first; I had already told him which questions needed to be done. After she left, Mitch read about half his assignment, and I questioned him about the reading. He knew every answer to the questions I asked.

*Analysis.*    When Betty told Robbie that we had looked at his report card, she asked what he thought and said that she thought he had done a great job. He replied that it was okay, but that he could do better so it wasn't that great. I think that his last report card has given him a lot of confidence in himself that was not there before. I especially think that the improvement in social studies has helped him in terms of his attitude toward schoolwork. Today I felt as if I were working with a completely different student. He seemed interested and excited about his work, and this was the first time I had heard him say that he would like to do well on something. Because Robbie was enthusiastic about doing well on this project, I think he learned more facts and he learned how interesting his subjects can be. I think that this type of assignment is exactly what Robbie needs. Most of the activities are short, fun, and easy. He also has immediate control over his grade because the point and grading scale were set up beforehand and were included in the packet. The final reason I think this is good for Robbie is that he has a month to work on it. I think that Robbie can do his work, but he probably works a lot slower than other kids. With his time schedule, I think Robbie can work at his own pace and still be able to complete enough of the activities to receive an A. In the following weeks I am going to check on Robbie's progress with this packet. I want to make sure he doesn't lose the enthusiasm about this assignment that he had today. Maybe doing well on this assignment will encourage him to work harder in other classes, too.

Today seemed to be a particularly difficult day with Mitch. I think that the problem was that I was being visibly irritated by Mitch's teacher, and he felt justified in showing his dislike for her. I felt that I would have tutored Mitch in the same manner whether or not she was instructing me; therefore, I thought her interruptions were merely taking time away from Mitch's study hall. I also didn't know how to respond to Mitch's attitude toward her. He said that the work he lied about would have been done if he had a different teacher at the school because that teacher was not mean. I think that Mitch wants to do the work, but he doesn't want to do it when she tells him to do it. Mitch wants to do anything she doesn't want him to do, and he'll only do the work when it gets to the point where it needs to be done in order for him to pass a test. Because we have been working on math, I wasn't able to ask Mitch about his previous readings. No matter what we work on next week, I will ask Mitch questions about this week's Civil War readings. Mitch should be getting the same packet as Robbie today, so I told him that it was fun and easy. After I described the whole assignment, he seemed eager to start working on it. He said that it sounded a lot better than doing chapter questions, but he didn't believe his teacher would give them such a creative assignment.

# Log for March 15

Time spent: 8:00–10:00 A.M.

### *Sequence of Events*

- Arrival
- Gym with music
- Light snack
- Storytelling
- Classwork on dinosaurs

*Episode(s).*    Today I went to the school in the morning so I could see what gym class was like and also participate in some of their "study" time. Carol informed me that today we would continue studying about dinosaurs and that eventually each student would write a paper or do some sort of presentation on what they had been learning over the past few weeks.

Last week the children made fossils of their handprints, so Carol started off the lesson by asking the children to review for me how a fossil is made. Cory explained that first an animal dies and then it decomposes. Then over a period of "thousands and millions and trillions of years" the bones get covered with mud and dirt and harden into fossils. Carol told Cory he was correct, except that it was only millions of years ago, not trillions, because no one was here at that time. Cory asked how Carol knew about a trillion years ago; and she responded, "You are right, Cory. I don't know about life a trillion years ago; it is a theory that scientists came up with."

Next Carol passed out a ditto on dinosaurs asking questions like: By looking at the footprints, which dinosaur do you think has the largest feet? Or, by looking at the teeth, which dinosaur do you think eats meat? Before she let the children begin, both Carol and I took around real animal skulls and asked the children to discuss what they saw. One skull was of a cow, another of a bird, and yet another a member of the cat family. The children carefully examined the teeth of each of the skulls and proclaimed that the ones with sharp teeth like the cat were meateaters and the ones with flat teeth or a long beak ate insects, berries, or seeds because these things did not need to be cut up. When I left to go to class they were to continue to discuss the different skulls.

*Analysis.*    My first impression was how quiet and attentive the children were during study time. I believe this is because the students are not only interested in the subject matter, but also because they all have a lot of respect for Carol as well. In fact, I have been noticing over the weeks that there is a strong relationship between Carol and all of the children. In part, this comes from the fact that the class size is small (there are two classes of about 13–15 kids each) and Carol has had some of the same children for two years already, but another part comes from the mutual respect and admiration Carol and her students have for one another. Last week Carol told me she cares about all of her students as if they were her own. This is evident by just watching her interact with the children, encouraging them, disciplining them, listening to them, and answering their questions. Although they are only children, Carol treats each of them as "mature young adults" and in return she expects and receives their respect and attention. (I realize this is a little out of place, but it is something I have observed over and over week after week in big and little ways.) Thus, Carol usually has little problem getting the students' attention.

The other aspect of Carol's teaching that I thought was extremely successful was her presentation. She began by reviewing, but more importantly she had real-life examples, that is, existing skulls for the children to look at. I remember that one of my goals for teaching this semester was to come up with fun and interesting ways to present the material and thus capture my students' attention. Carol is extremely talented in this area. Whereas this week we used real-life skulls, last week they used clay to make fossils, and the week before we all made dinosaur mobiles. As I saw with the use of the skulls, these different approaches truly capture the students' interest. They were all fascinated by the skulls, and each student called me over so he or she could meticulously examine the teeth and details of each of the animals. In addition, use of these hands-on materials were far better attention holders than Carol or myself simply talking at them.

Finally, Carol's answer to Cory about the trillions of years ago I thought was also impressive. I have never heard Carol say, "You are wrong" or "Because I say so," etc. In this case, Carol told Cory he was right: There was no way she could know about a trillion years ago for sure, but scientists who have studied the earth and fossils have a theory about how old the earth is and, although nobody knows for sure, they think it is less than a trillion years old. Cory was satisfied with this answer and Carol had given him a fair explanation.

I really enjoy watching Carol teach the children. I think she is an excellent teacher and besides teaching the students she often takes the time to explain her actions and decisions to me as well. I am definitely learning a lot about the "art of teaching" this semester!

## Log for March 6 and March 10

Time spent: 12:00–1:00 P.M.

### *Sequence of Events*

Monday: Fifth period I worked with Lin in her study hall and helped her complete a lab for her science class. Sixth period I worked with Amanda in the library and we did some research for an English project.

Friday: Fifth period I worked on a reading assignment with Lin in her study hall. We read segments of the book *Cheaper by the Dozen* and then answered questions on a ditto. Sixth period I worked with Amanda in the library on her states and capitals.

***Episodes.*** Friday afternoon, Lin and I worked on her reading assignment. She had partially completed the ditto during class, but she still had several questions that she needed to answer. These questions were based on sections of the book that she had already read in her reading class; however, we would usually reread the specific section in the book to refresh her memory. We worked by ourselves at one of the round tables in the classroom. There was one other student in the classroom during this period and he was working with the aide at the other round table.

One section of the book that we read was about four pages long. This section described how the father of the family (the family consisted of 12 children) attempted to make his children math wizards. He was a very mathematical person himself and wanted to pass on his tricks to his children. So, every night at dinner he would quiz the children extensively. First they learned their multiplication tables, and then he taught them an elaborate method for multiplying two large numbers together in their heads. The book went into a fair degree of detail at this point and specifically described the method that he taught them. Lin read all of this section out loud to me. While she read, she held the book fairly close to her face. She also read in a monotone most of the time. About half of the time she would pause at commas and periods to show the phrasing, and the other half of the time she would just continue right on. The only time she stopped reading was to ask me the meaning of the word *ludicrous*. After we finished reading this section, she went to the ditto and read the question, "How did the Gilbreth children become math wizards?" She usually would answer the questions verbally before she wrote anything: "Well, they took one number and subtracted it from 50, I think, and then what did they do? Oh, I think they had to square it, maybe, and add it to another number? The other number had to do with 25 . . . I don't know . . . I don't understand . . . how am I supposed to answer this?" At this point I explained to her that the math was very difficult, but that I didn't think they were specifically asking us to explain the math. I suggested that we read the question again. Then I rephrased the question. "So how did the kids get to be so good at math?"

"Well . . . from their father, I guess. . ."

"And what did he do?"

"Oh, no, . . . do I have to go through all those rules again?" As she said this, Lin rolled her eyes.

*Analysis.*    This episode gave me some indication of the problems Lin has with reading comprehension. The first clue came when she was reading the book out loud to me. She had read this section in class, so she already knew the story. However, if I hadn't known that she had already read it once, I would have thought it was her first time reading it. Although she read the words fine, she did not give any "color" to the story. She didn't raise her voice to indicate questions, she frequently did not pause at the ends of phrases, etc. As she read, I wondered whether she really understood what she was reading. It seemed like she was just reading the words on the page. This observation suggested to me that the mere act of reading takes most of her concentration. It doesn't seem like she is able to think much about what she is actually reading.

The second clue as to the nature of her difficulties came when she attempted to answer the question. Lin's first answer to the question indicated that she had understood some of what she had read. She understood that they were trying to do math. However, she seemed to have missed the big picture of the story, that the father spent much time at dinner every night teaching his children mathematical tricks. Instead, she got caught up in the details, trying to understand exactly how the math tricks worked.

Having learned about Lin's weaknesses in reading, I would treat such an assignment differently in the future. I would still have her read the passage herself, because I think it is an important skill to be able to read something and understand what was read. However, instead of going right to the question when she finished reading, I would first have her tell me, in her own words, what she had just read. In this manner, I would hope to help her develop the ability to step back, think about what she read, and develop an overall picture of the story in her mind. Then she could take this overall understanding with her and tackle the questions.

## Log for February 6

Time spent: 6:30 P.M.–9:00 P.M.

### *Sequence of Events*

- I arrive at adult learning center and speak to Margaret about the agenda of the class.
- The class arrives, and the new students whom I had not yet met introduce themselves.
- I observe Margaret as she reviews with the class several handouts of common English idioms.
- Margaret divides the class into pairs, gives each pair a scenario, and asks each pair to construct and present a telephone conversation dealing with that scenario.
- Each pair presents their conversation to the class. Class ends.

***Episodes.***  When we returned from break Margaret split the class into five pairs. Because there were only nine students in the class that night, Margaret requested, if I didn't mind, that I be Kim's partner for this exercise. I immediately said yes, and when I took my chair over to where Kim was sitting, she smiled slightly and I smiled back. I did not know much about her except that she was from China, about 40 years old, and that she was a physician in her country.

Margaret then gave Kim and me, as well as the other pairs, a scenario from which we were to create a short telephone conversation and present that conversation to the class. Our scenario involved two people, person A asking person B if B would like to come to dinner at A's home. I asked Kim if she would like to be person A or B and she said, "I think that I would prefer A." I responded, "Cool. You're A then and I'll be B." She nodded her head and took out a pencil and a blank piece of paper.

We began to construct our conversation, and I encouraged Kim to use the idioms that we had practiced earlier in class. After the greetings of "Hello" and "How are you?" Kim said, "I want to know if you want to eat dinner on March 18?" After I heard this sentence, I asked Kim if she knew of any other way to build this sentence, and if there were any idioms in English that could replace any of the phrases in her sentence. She looked through her list of idioms and tried the sentence again, saying, "I wonder if you wanted to eat dinner at my house on March 18?" I said, "Terrific. You put 'wonder' in place of 'want to know.' Is there anything else? How about 'to eat dinner at my house'?" Kim glanced at her idiom handout again, and shook her head, saying that she didn't know what else to replace it with. Realizing that it wasn't on her sheet, I wrote on her paper, "*come over* to my house *for* dinner." She nodded, said, "Oh, yes," and then repeated, "I was wondering if you wanted to come over to my house for dinner on March 18?" I smiled broadly and said, "Absolutely! What time should I come over?" She quickly replied, "Six o'clock," and I answered, "Six o'clock sounds great. I'm looking forward to it." "Me, too," said Kim, smiling. "Bye," she said, and I answered, "Take care!" After that, Kim wrote down the entire conversation and we presented it to the class.

***Analysis.***    Although she was never very outspoken in class, I found out through working with Kim that she absorbed information like a sponge. She rarely said things correctly the first time, but once she was corrected, the material was fortified in her mind. I was truly amazed by the quickness of Kim's learning and her *strategies* for learning the language. She was not afraid to make mistakes, but once she did, she worked diligently on correcting them. I admired that in her and by watching her work and absorb these bits of language, I began to think about my own strategies of teaching the language. I realize now that there is a central commonality between her learning and my teaching process.

Her strategy and my strategy came out naturally. Not naturally as a natural talent; rather, naturally as a smooth, connected process that is not necessarily consciously thought about. For example, I don't think that Kim actually knows while she is in the process of learning exactly what her learning strategy is. I saw her strategy as repetition coupled with a concentration on the important parts of the sentence. But did she realize her strategy?—I don't think she did. Maybe after the fact, but not during the learning process.

I am the same way! While I was teaching her about the new idioms, questioning and challenging her while trying not to discourage her, I just did it. I didn't really think about what I was doing. It was only after the fact that I even thought about how I helped her to find the right idioms and encouraged her to finish the conversation. I didn't plan on giving her such a warm smile, but that smile worked, causing her to feel comfortable enough to continue with the conversation. What did I do right? Well, I can see it now. But it's so difficult to assess your own strategy while you're actually involved with the teaching and learning process.

We talked in class about the need to constantly reevaluate our work. In fact, our whole class is focused on the reflective approach to field experience, about taking the time to assess those things that we did or didn't do, to change, enhance, tear apart, whatever. What I am concerned about is the time when I am actually teaching. How can I assess when I'm completely focused on the teaching itself? The teaching and learning process, at least in my opinion, comes out so naturally, so freely, and so completely that I can't assess as I teach or learn. I must take time like this to assess after or before the fact. Is this okay? Is self-assessment sufficient if we do it only after or before we teach and learn? Perhaps I should try to incorporate some self-assessment into my teaching style. Will that help me improve?

Next week I'd like to focus a bit on the way I teach, *while* I'm teaching. How do I approach the students? How do I respond to their questions? Are my strategies effective? The more I think about it, the more I feel that it's important not to go on autopilot in the classroom and then think about it later.

## SAMPLE PROGRESS REPORTS

## The Bay City Community Center

EILEEN LAUREANO

BCCC, or the Bay City Community Center, is a cultural and activities center for children and young adults. Most of the children who attend its afterschool program are students from nearby King Elementary School. These children are there primarily because their parents are still working when school ends at 3 o'clock and cannot be picked up until 5 o'clock. Without any other alternative these children would go home alone to vegetate in front of the television set. BCCC provides them with activities, including "the winning edge," the homework room; MAC, the games and crafts room; the computer room; gym, science room, art room, and playground.

BCCC also runs other programs for these children who need individualized attention. The one in which I participated is called the "Special Kid Project." Children selected for this program are those who recently have developed emotional or social problems, either at home or school, that have affected their development. The interns for this program are selected to provide personalized attention for these children and to help them overcome some of their difficulties. The process involves being their role model and teacher by giving advice and providing discipline, and stimulating social interaction by exposing these children to different BCCC activities as well as to other children.

The child I worked with in the Special Kid Project was Alison, a 6-year-old girl who had arrived in Bay City in November and as yet had not made any friends. She is also the child of divorced parents. She has two brothers. Her favorite and the one she misses the most lives with her father down south. Her 10-year-old brother, also a child in the Special Kid Project, lives with her, to her disappointment. He is extremely rude and obnoxious with everyone, but especially with his sister Alison. Alison's main problem is that she has developed poor social skills. She is often too blunt and frank to the point of being rude, and is usually very quiet and distant among other children. Most of the time she refuses to play with other children and, as a result, has caused many children to reject her. Her behavior is said to have been learned in large part from her mother, who is just as rude, if not more, and is thus disliked by many adults as well.

---

Names of people, places, and schools have been changed in order to protect the privacy of those involved.

At the beginning of my field experience the most important goals I set out for myself were to be self-motivated and to develop confidence in what I was doing. I wanted to be able to establish plans and goals and carry them out completely. My field experience modified this goal for me. I realized it was unrealistic to go into an assignment with a set plan as if it were a syllabus set in stone. Humans are flexible and our moods vary frequently, especially in children. I realize also that my plans can be developed most effectively by the child. By observing and listening to what the child wants and needs, I can most effectively develop plans that best satisfy the child's needs. Thus, my new goal is to set goals day by day and allow flexibility for change.

Overcoming my fear and apprehension of the unknown was one of the goals I most needed to work on. Having never done anything similar to this, which seemed to require so much skill and responsibility, made me hesitant about whether I could actually perform my duties well. Going into the experience I decided to dive in and whatever happened happened. Talking with the other volunteers I realized we shared the same fears and the only way to overcome them was to *take one day at a time.* Working with Alison helped subdue some of these apprehensions and helped me realize that my main objective was to learn. Whether or not I made mistakes, my involvement in the program was going to be an excellent learning experience for both of us.

Developing Alison's social skills and emotional stability was probably the most important goal of the program. However, I seriously did not believe that someone as inexperienced as I was could make any kind of difference in this little girl's life. In fact, I felt sorry that she ended up with a volunteer who probably had similar problems as a child and who had found very few answers in attempting to overcome them until reaching adulthood. I realize now that I was not necessarily as inexperienced as I thought, having learned quite a bit from my nine-year-old brother. I also believe that the few weeks I spent with her were not spent in vain, and will provide a good starting point for her continued development and an excellent foundation for my interest in teaching.

My field experience as a Special Kid Project intern taught me many thing about teaching. However, it taught me more than what I could ever learn from textbooks. It taught me how to listen and learn from children in order to understand the many and sometimes complicated reasons for their behavior. I learned to examine my own biases before making judgments in order to reduce false assumptions about children's behaviors. In comparing one child with another I learned how their differences work to help or hinder their development. Most importantly for me, I learned how the methods one uses to get certain results from a child can unexpectedly and accidently change, providing better results than anything preplanned. Essentially, what I learned was flexibility both to learn and experiment.

One of the first things I learned soon after my initial introduction to Alison was overcoming my own biases about childish behavior. Going into this program I held my own beliefs on why children throw tantrums, pout, or get upset. Coming from a home with a spoiled nine-year-old who screams and yells every time he wants his way made me generalize what I believe is "brattish" and spoiled behavior to all children. As adults we tend to view children not as small "people" but as "brats" or babies. We fail to realize that they, too, can have bad experiences that can affect their moods. Knowing this, I have become aware that I have negative assumptions about childish behavior. I realized that I have to remove these blinders before I can effectively "listen" to a child and understand why he or she reacts or feels a certain way. False assumptions such as this may not only affect my judgment, but may also interfere with the development of effective responsive methods.

What helped me reflect on the effects of my biases was an incident at one of our earliest meetings. On that day Alison had shown a lot of initiative and motivation by voluntarily trying some of BCCC's many activities. Suddenly, however, her mood changed while playing. As the game progressed, she began to pout and stomp her feet on the base, saying she was bored because she hated playing second base. When asked why, she responded that she could never tag anyone out. Despite my attempts to motivate her by pointing out children her own age who were playing and contentedly learning the game, she continued to whine, kick, and throw herself on the floor.

A similar incident occurred later when Alison was faced with the possibility of playing with Stacey. She adamantly refused to play with her and began to cry at the idea. However, after further questioning, I learned Stacey had kicked Alison earlier. At both of these incidents I first reacted with frustration as I tried to figure out ways to make her comply with me, not throw tantrums, and stop crying. I then realized that a person's mood or behavior, even a child's emotions, has its causes. By continuing to talk with her, I realized she had very valid reasons for being upset or angry that day. I discarded my initial assumptions, realizing that my biases had hindered my attempts to find a cause and hence a solution to her behavior.

Assumptions such as this can also arise in a classroom setting. Here it may present an even greater problem because of the greater number of students. Overgeneralizing the causes of certain behaviors to so many students can further distance the teacher from the student and therefore reduce his or her ability to remedy emotional or behavioral conflicts. The diversified personalities of the students would also require the teacher to tailor his or her method of conflict resolution to each student.

Another valuable learning experience taught me the advantages of listening in identifying potential problems in children. Listening for both the child and adult teacher can help one understand the causes of a child's dilemma. A simple secret I learned was to "ask." Children are very open and honest and usually will tell you exactly what they feel. Also, by asking people about the child who know the child very well, one can gain a different perspective and insight into the child's life and conflicts. Understanding the problem from all points of view provides a sound basis for drawing conclusions and formulating effective methods or theories for overcoming challenging social and emotional difficulties.

An insightful incident that brought this idea into perspective for me occurred as I was successfully attempting to engage in more personal conversation with Alison. My main concern was getting to know Alison on a more personal level. While in a relaxed atmosphere on the swings she began telling me about her family, especially her brother, and her relationship with them. I learned her parents are divorced and her father has custody of her favorite brother. She told me she is unable to communicate with him because her father lives down south and does not have a phone. The brother she does not get along with lives with her.

While continuing to talk with her, however, I tried to motivate her to play with some girls nearby. Alison asked to play, but was regrettably ignored and rejected. She walked away saddened and hurt. As I began to leave for the day, I noticed she was following me in. I told her to remain playing, but sadly she replied she had no friends to play with.

When I asked the coordinator about Alison's feelings, she confirmed that Alison had developed no real friendships since her arrival in November. She informed me Alison lacked some of the "social graces" needed to interact with others. She often can be too frank or blunt to the point of being rude. It is suspected she learned this maladaptive behavior from her mother, who I am told is the same way.

Listening and communicating with children and adults is also applicable in the classroom. However, both of these factors require a lot of personalized attention, which may be difficult to achieve because of the large size of most classrooms. The teacher can still achieve some of this private interaction by dividing children into small groups, attending parent-teacher meetings, holding one-on-one conferences, and participating in "open house" activities.

An unfortunate change of plans in my project, which was at first disappointing, turned into a valuable learning experience. By suddenly and surprisingly changing the child I was working with, I was able to observe and contrast the similarities and differences between two 6-year-old girls. Through these observations I learned how different personalities in children can affect their relationships with their peers.

This particular learning occurred when Alison was suddenly and mysteriously pulled out of BCCC. I was then assigned another 6-year-old girl, Jill, who was not involved in the Special Kid Project. My initial reaction was, "What can I possibly do for a child with no apparent problems?" To my surprise, I discovered a lot; primarily, I learned how differences in social interactions can affect the development of friendships. Jill was the exact opposite of Alison. Whereas Alison was quiet and often rude, Jill was talkative and friendly. Jill would spend a long time telling me about her day, making funny faces at me, and laughing. Jill's friendliness and talkativeness were examples of a more secure and stable child's behavior.

Although it may be unfair or inappropriate to compare Alison and Jill, each child, at least on the surface, showed how one's social behavior affects the responses one receives from others. Alison's quiet and sometimes rude behavior resulted in many children rejecting her. As a result, she had few if any friends. Jill's quick smile and friendliness made her easily approachable and fun to be with. She had no problems finding other children to play with. In fact, many children often sought her out to play.

Comparing children, however, may not be applicable to every situation. Comparing children, especially in classrooms where there are so many different children and personalities, can result in an overgeneralization of how the model child should behave. This may result in the development of false expectations and inappropriate behavior on the part of the teacher when these expectations are not met. Although, if done carefully, by examining the characteristics of the average child, the teacher may be able to pick out extraneous differences in children that may well present a problem. Such problems might include dyslexia, maladaptive behaviors, "special" children, and emotional disturbances.

Finally, one of the most important things I learned through my field experience was that lack of attention may actually be more effective in getting desired results that showering a child with too much attention. This is especially true if a child knows he or she will get a favorable response if he or she whines or throws a tantrum. The child will not seek to change this maladaptive behavior. By changing one's usual response to a particular behavior, one may halt the maladaptive behavior and force the child to assume a more sociable behavior.

The incident that helped me realize this occurred during a game involving Alison and another child. Alison and I began a game of "Sorry," and after a while a boy named Larry appeared wanting to play also. Alison refused to play if Larry was allowed to play. Despite my attempts to suggest that it would be more fun if more people played, she adamantly refused. Pouting and whining, she demanded I go outside and play with her. I was forced to choose whether to ignore Larry or ignore Alison's selfish attitude. Rather than give in to Alison, I refused and continued to play with Larry. She then stormed out. I felt a bit guilty for ignoring her, but to my surprise she returned after just a few minutes. She sat on my lap and began to play my card for me. By playing my cards she was in effect playing with Larry.

This event was particularly surprising because I always assumed the best thing for Alison was attention. Giving her attention, however, never changed her behavior. Ignoring her or not giving her any attention actually worked and made her play with another child. Realizing that she was not going to get her way forced her to change her antisocial attitude. This helped fulfill our goal to help her learn to play with others.

Withdrawing attention rather than giving attention can definitely be applied to other situations. Children often will whine, shout, or stomp in attempts to draw attention to themselves and get what they want. Oftentimes they will receive that attention because adults want them to stop or keep quiet. We usually do not realize that by doing so we encourage their disruptive behavior rather than discourage it. In addition, when other children see that this type of behavior gets them what they want, they will also attempt to mimic it. A teacher may then have to divide his or her attention among 20 or more students—an almost impossible task. Hence, sometimes in order to get a desired behavior from a child one needs to reduce the attention given. Once the child realizes that he or she will not get any attention, he or she will conform to the more appropriate behavior.

Reflecting back on some of my goals, I believe I have successfully accomplished some of them, while failing to accomplish others. Entering my first teaching experience like most novices, I was fearful of what I did not know. I was also extremely insecure about what was expected of me and whether I could successfully fulfill the program's expectations. This apprehension at the start was due in large part to my lack of experience in working with children nearly four times younger than I was. My only experience with children had been baby-sitting my younger brother. However, I know my sibling and what to expect from him. I did not know Alison. I was afraid she would reject me, not want me to tag along with her, or be so much of a problem that I would not know how to handle her. Growing up in a predominantly black and Hispanic area, I was never exposed to children of another ethnic group or culture. Thus, I was also unsure of what to expect from a white six-year-old child. I did not know whether she would view me as different or whether I would view her as different from me. I wondered if I should do anything differently because of our backgrounds and, if so, what. As I soon learned, children are the same everywhere; they cry, play, whine, fight, and love all the same way. My perceptions of any differences between us because of culture or ethnicity soon faded, as well as my apprehension about age differences. The children there provided not only a learning experience for me but entertainment as well.

I believe that I fulfilled some of the expectations of the Special Kid Project program. One of the first goals was to establish a good rapport with Alison. I wanted to provide a relaxing and friendly atmosphere in which I could gain her trust. In establishing a trusting relationship I was able to learn more about her background, her family, and her feelings. She also became comfortable enough with me to approach me freely and suggest and teach me new games to play.

One of the most important goals of the program was to develop Alison's social skills and better develop her emotional stability while increasing her interaction with other children. This goal was to be accomplished by exposing her to all the different activities at BCCC in the hopes that she would find something of interest to her and consequently establish a friendship with someone who shared similar interests. Although upon finishing my fieldwork experience this goal had not been completely fulfilled, I feel that I had made some progress, however minor. I believe that given more time and more assistance, Alison will be able to strengthen her social skills and development.

One of my major accomplishments is the fact that I was successful in getting her to try more of the BCCC activities, including the game room, art room, gym, science room, and the "winning edge." Even though she was only briefly exposed to some of these activities, it is hoped that she will continue to utilize them at her leisure and interest. I also believe that she was beginning to make some progress in terms of showing some initiative in talking and playing with children. On one occasion I was proud of the fact that she had approached other girls at play and had slowly tried to join them. Alison finally managed to get enough nerve to ask them if she could play. Unfortunately, they did not respond positively toward Alison and simply ignored her. I only hope that she continues to show that same initiative despite minor setbacks. Alison can succeed as long as she keeps trying and gives others the opportunity to know her.

Before I left, Alison had begun to play with other children. Although she was stubbornly unwilling to attempt to play with another child, I had somehow managed to get her to play. By refusing to accept a "No" from Alison I was able to withdraw my attention from her, thus forcing her to accept my ideas. On that day she played extensively and joined in conversation with Larry. This event can also stimulate her to become more involved in activities, especially games. Alison can then realize that by being more responsive to other children instead of stubbornly running away, she can sharpen her social skills, thereby allowing herself the opportunity to develop friends.

One goal that I failed to accomplish was helping Alison overcome her rude and often cold behavior toward other children. Her behavior is one of the main reasons she lacks any real friendships. Any attempt by another child to interact with her in any way was immediately turned off upon the child's listening or being with Alison. I had hopes of really getting her to change her behavior more than just on one particular day. I wanted her to become friendly and open on a daily basis. My failure to accomplish this goal was primarily due to the brief time I was able to spend with her. She definitely needs someone to spend more time with her developing her social skills. I was also unable to help her as much simply because I lacked some of the skills needed to work with such a child. There were many times when I was left with no answers or solutions to any of her problems. This was especially frustrating when I realized how hurt she was at not having any friends to play with other than myself. I really did not have all the answers to everything, but perhaps no one does.

Whether the brief changes I saw in Alison will continue or become just exceptions to her behavior, I do not know. I only hope that my brief experience with her can make even a small dent for someone else to continue and improve upon. However, Alison was able to teach me many more and valuable things, including patience, tolerance, confidence, and above all how to listen. Employing all of these valuable skills, I was able to learn a small sampling of what teaching truly requires. I will take these skills with me as I continue to explore the teaching profession, and hopefully I will eventually become a more effective teacher for it.

## The Special Program School

MINDY ZANE

*Context.*    The Special Program School (SPS) is a middle/high school combination that sits just above the main intersection in downtown Elm City. "But what makes it a *Special* school?" is the question I heard most frequently from inquiring friends and colleagues. My answer was usually as follows: It's a school for students who are not interested in or attracted to the traditional school that most of us are used to. It's kind of like the school in *Fame,* although it doesn't concentrate on the arts. It's not only for "gifted" students, although there are some of them there, and it's not only for "at-risk" students, but there are some of them there, too.

The SPS has democracy at its core. Within its walls one finds the old American tradition of the town meeting. The students are involved in the administrative decisions as well as in deciding which classes they would like to take. "Family groups" and "morning meetings" characterize the SPS. Also, the students don't receive grades here, only evaluations. One cannot help noticing the unique atmosphere at the SPS, and when I heard a tutor was needed in Spanish, I jumped at the opportunity. A "less conservative" style of teaching was what I was interested in and the SPS was where that was at.

Murals cover the walls, recycling bins sit at the entrance, and students' projects decorate the halls. The teachers walk around in sneakers and sweatshirts, and the students wear everything from tie-dyes, to Birkenstocks, to tight leggings. The classes are small (average of about ten students?) and the atmosphere is communal. Thursdays have recently become "Activity Day," and as I arrive, students are leaving with different teachers—carrying tennis rackets, wearing hiking boots, or walking bicycles.

Although my "supervisor" is Janet Hamilton, I am basically on my own. I work with Richy Walters, a senior, who needs help with second cycle Spanish more or less in order to graduate. We meet two mornings a week for a total of about 2½ hours in a teacher's office, but not in the literal sense of "office." I observed Richy's Spanish class in progress only once—usually it's just he and I.

***Goals.*** Flexibility is key. That's what I've learned over the past few months. Originally, I had two goals for my field experience. First and foremost, I wanted Richy to pass Spanish II and not have it keep him from graduating. But I also let my idealistic nature contribute to my goals and I wanted Richy to understand Spanish, to *think* about the subject instead of just do the assignments.

On a less conscious level, I think that I also wanted to be someone who made a difference in his life, someone who made schoolwork exciting instead of tedious. But all along I kept thinking, "Is this what I want to do with my life?" "Do I really want to be a teacher?" In other words, I wanted this experience to make my future a little bit clearer.

***Learning Through Episodes.*** I think that the most controversial part of my field experience has been the conflict between creative, inspirational learning and doing only what needs to be done in order to satisfy requirements for the class. The nature of tutoring in itself is restrictive. An incident that I had with one of the teachers at the SPS made me describe my situation as being "trapped in a completely closed curriculum." That is, I was only there to get Richy through the semester, not to shed any creative light onto the scene or to decide what *I* thought he should learn. When I briefly touched on this issue with Richy's math teacher, the response was, "Just help him do his homework and pass the class."

This is an issue that many teachers throughout the nation must face because of standardized testing and national exams. In a way, everyone is in some sort of trap because of guidelines that must be met or quotas that must be filled. Stanford Achievement Tests and Regents are examples of tests that students must take and, therefore, the teacher has the responsibility to prepare the students for those tests. It's a complicated sort of catch-22: A teacher is judged by how well his or her students do on tests, and yet at times the tests are products of something other than the teachers!

Before I get tangled up in my own words, I want to bring up an answer that I found to this situation. Although at times we are victims of a mandatory curriculum, we—as teachers—do have the opportunity to cover that material in a variety of ways. That is, I discovered that creativity is an essential part of the learning process. At times Richy was bored or at least unenthusiastic about Spanish. So throughout the semester I used an assortment of different methods to cover what had to be learned. One example that sticks in my mind is a "Cultural Tidbit" that Richy had to translate in his Spanish book. The narrative was a generalization about vacations in Spain and it covered an area near Barcelona called the "Costa Brava."

Well, as it turns out, I studied in Spain last semester and I have vivid memories about going down that very coast on a train from Paris. I asked Richy if he was interested in knowing more about the place, and he said that he was. The agreement could have been a stalling tactic on his part but, if the procrastination involved talking about Spanish topics, I was in favor of it. Anyway, I told him why the region was Catalonian instead of Castilian, what the water of the Mediterranean looked like when the sun was coming up behind it, and other details about Spain. He was so impressed with the fact that I had been there. I drew him maps of the country and answered all of his questions about the people, the social life, the food, etc. Giving Richy a context for what he was learning became a very important issue. Whether it was comparing the grammar to examples in English that he understood or explaining that "Esteban" was really "Steven," I tried to add a little bit of reality to what we were doing. The creativity factor went beyond that, though. I also used role playing, charades, and other games to pull him through the lessons. At times I would jump out of my chair and run out of the room only to make him understand the Spanish verb "to return." He would throw back his head and laugh about his crazy tutor who was "acting for him."

Besides being creative, I learned how important flexibility is in education. I could never have a lesson plan because we would just do whatever Richy needed to get done for the class. In the beginning, I was nervous as hell and completely without confidence. I needed to know ahead of time what we would be going over, and I even wanted to photocopy the pages in his book so that I could go over the material before I helped him. Well, that lasted about a week. I realized that I really *did* know the material and that I had the knowledge just to help him with whatever happened to be assigned.

But flexibility was more than doing each session "cold turkey." It also meant being able to read Richy's verbal and nonverbal signals and understand when he wasn't comprehending the material or when he was just plain sick of doing Spanish. He had a habit of looking out the window and rubbing his hands together when his mind was drifting. He also loved to slither out of a question or a reading by asking me to do it or saying that he wanted to hear me read first. I began to realize that if he was to understand anything, we had to use moderation.

That brings up another issue—retention. That same teacher that I mentioned before said that Richy had "a learning disability, I suppose." I wasn't sure what the exact psychological term should have been but I knew that he definitely took a long time to digest the material. This made me realize how critical it was to be patient. I would *never* be visibly upset or disappointed with him because he was taking too long with an assignment. Not even that, at times he would look at a topic that we had covered thoroughly the week before and act as if he had never seen the concept before. I calmly reminded him what we had discovered the last time and hopefully the material would come back to him.

Another issue that I was confronted with a few times during the fieldwork was the fact that I had to trust Richy implicitly when it came to how he did on a test or how everything was going in the classroom. One time, he completely avoided the fact that he failed a test—he hadn't even told me that he was having one to begin with! I suppose that I could have gone to his teacher and found out his progress on my own, but that didn't seem fair to me. Richy and I respected each other and I felt that he should be the one to inform me. In a way, I could have been jeopardizing his improvement by relying only on his word, but what is the *right* thing to do in that kind of situation? I find it very difficult to believe that he would have turned over a new academic leaf because I was checking up on him. Maybe I just think that part of the responsibility is his and that he had to be the link between me and the classroom.

I had the opportunity one day to sit in on his Spanish class and that experience created an entirely new dilemma in my mind. Seeing Richy in the context of a classroom with other students made me compare them in a way that I know is wrong. The SPS doesn't "track" their students at all. I, on the other hand, am a product of a completely tracked school system. Students were labeled and taught accordingly. Only recently, with this class and fieldwork, have I been able to see the error in that way of thinking. What happens when we classify and categorize children? Sociologists who have studied teachers' behaviors with students of varying socioeconomic backgrounds have found that, "depending on how they categorize a student, teachers apply different rules, employ different sanctions when students break rules, have different academic and occupational expectations, apply different academic standards, seek different amounts of student input in instructional decision making, allocate different amounts of instructional time, and teach different content."[1] We can be creating self-fulfilling prophecies by telling them that they are at a "basic skills" level or "honors" students. I really need to experience classroom life that at the SPS more in order to figure out this problem. I mean, I am not really sure *how* one goes about *not* tracking students.

***Generalizability.*** Given the distinct nature of a tutoring type of situation, I have difficulty with sweeping generalizations about my teaching experience. However, a few common ideals emerged throughout my field experience, some of which were mentioned in the previous section. Obviously, I've had no experience with different students who have varying needs. Richy spoiled me, in that sense. However, concepts such as creativity, flexibility, understanding, and patience seem to be characteristics, or at least should be characteristics, of any teaching situation. Education is definitely a two-way street. Teachers wouldn't get very far without students, and students would be virtually lost without teachers. In other words, I hope to remember the qualities that I have discovered as essential components of this process that we call education.

However, the uniqueness of the fieldwork made me somewhat of a stranger to the concepts introduced by the texts and other readings. "Foundational studies" and the "six basic teaching issues" were more ideas on paper than actual components of my experience. While I see myself at a small disadvantage for not gaining "typical" teaching experience, I realized the point that a "typical" teaching experience does not really exist.

***Goal Achievement.*** Well, although our college releases its students in the middle of May, the Special Program School keeps its children for at least another month. That means that I am not sure about the status of my first goal in the field experience. I honestly don't know if Richy is going to graduate or not. When I was home over spring break, my mother asked me how the tutoring was going. She said, "Are you going to pass him?" I nearly lost it right there. Perhaps the biggest dilemma of all has been the battle that I have been having with myself about Richy's fate. I can only do so much. I can walk him through a homework assignment and play guessing games in order to remember vocabulary but I cannot sit beside him in the classroom. Two-way street, remember? The power of a teacher seems to go only so far. The rest is up to the student.

I simply cannot blame myself if he doesn't make it this semester. What else could I have done, given the situation? Although this field experience course culminates with this paper, my time with Richy can't end right now. I will be here in Elm City this summer and I will continue going to the SPS as long as I can. I start training for a summer job up here during the second week of June, but Richy has school until the 24th or so. I will do my best.

On another level, I *do* think that I have done something for Richy Walters. He doesn't fake his excitement when he holds up a completed page of homework. He isn't bullshitting me when he tells me how much my tutoring means to him. And he doesn't *hate* Spanish. In a small way, I think that he understands the whole subject a little bit better. Maybe he won't recall the preterit form of the verb "to run" in the third person singular, but I have a feeling he'll remember how proud Spanish families are and how beautiful the beaches are in Spain. But there is that dilemma again—what if the beauty of the beaches doesn't cut it for the final exam? Ugh.

As far as my personal situation goes, I learned that my future has the potential to be very exciting. I also realized that charades won't work when students don't want to play the game. It was a very exciting, very scary realization—the whole field experience, that is. So much of education these days is discipline and I didn't have to deal with any of that with Richy. I stuck my toe in the water during the field experience. One day, I will have to just jump right in.

## Marshall Youth Lacrosse Program

### A. GABRIEL AUBLE

*Context.*   The Marshall Youth Bureau is the main local government branch responsible for organizing and delivering youth athletics to children in the Marshall community. Included in the youth athletic programs is the Youth Lacrosse Program that is run by the former Marshall High School lacrosse coach. Coach Harris believes that good lacrosse players and a successful high school team result from children being involved in "playing" lacrosse, not just watching it.

I ran into Coach Harris before the season began, and he told me about the program and asked if I would be interested in volunteer coaching. As a former player of Coach Harris's and a lover of lacrosse, I became very excited about the idea and went to the organizational meeting. It was here that I got a glimpse of the target group to whom we would be delivering our program. The volunteer coaches were all very affluent professionals: a doctor, the owner of a travel agency, a couple of lawyers, the vice-president of a local bank, and the former high school principal. All of the coaches had a son or nephew in the program. In discussing how teams would be broken up, I learned that several of the children who would be in the program also played hockey, an expensive sport to participate in, especially for growing children.

I was assigned as head coach of twelve 9- to 12-year-olds with an assistant coach to help me out. We met twice a week at 5 o'clock on Wednesdays and 2 o'clock on Sundays at the Marshall High School playing fields. The first day, it looked as if every child had one or both parents present or the child was with a family friend, and most children were white. During future meetings many parents came to watch the children on a regular basis or at least to pick them up to take them home. Judging by the energy and excitement of the kids and conversations with my three participating nephews from the first practice onward, it was obvious that the kids were there because they wanted to be there; it was fun for them. I was there by choice as well; I love lacrosse and I love children. It was great to coach/teach under these circumstances.

*Goals.* My personal goals for this experience were simple: to get experience teaching and interacting with a group of young children, to test my ability to teach kids, and to have them like me as a coach and friend. Also, I wanted this experience to give me some insight as to the type of children and in what context I would like to teach in the future.

The goals I had for the kids were consistent with those outlined by Coach Harris. They were: (1) Players should learn the basics of lacrosse in an enjoyable, safe atmosphere. (2) Players should learn to compete on an individual and a team basis with a healthy attitude toward wins and losses, not a "winning is everything" attitude. (3) Players should learn to pass and catch efficiently. (4) Players should benefit from positive contact with adult coaches.

Finally, the goals I had as a coach were to make sure I was a consistent, positive leader at every game and practice; to encourage teamwork through passing, helping on defense if someone got beat by his or her opponent, and talking/communication on the field between teammates; to make sure all players got equal playing time and played all positions; to help individuals develop and improve passing and catching skills, defensive and offensive play, and cultivate individual strengths such as speed or strength; and to ensure an atmosphere that was safe and enjoyable for the players.

*Learning.* I believe that effective teaching results not only from the teacher's motivation and enthusiasm about the subject matter, but is heavily dependent on the children's motivation to be present and learn the subject matter, and the atmosphere in which lessons are taught. Yet, it is also necessary for the teacher to genuinely care for the learners and to demonstrate care through positive verbal feedback, including smiles and pats on the back. Furthermore, I strongly believe that parental support of the child's participation in an activity greatly affects that child's success or feelings of success in the activity.

Effective lessons are the result of the teacher's knowledge of the subject matter and the teacher's preparation for the lesson, whether thought out or written out, and the delivery style of the lesson by the teacher, for example, modeling, lecturing, or active learner involvement. A good lesson is also one that focuses on the learners and their skill levels and cognitive comprehension levels. This may be the most difficult part of teaching, but, fortunately, when teaching a basic skill, both the beginners and advanced learners benefit from practice.

Giving constant positive feedback to the learner is one crucial teaching skill. The teacher must be able to always find a way to praise the learner's actions, yet not let the child become complacent with himself/herself. This means saying things like, "You did a really good job today, but what could you have done better, or how do you think you can improve even more next time?" My learners really responded well to this type of questioning when I asked what they thought needed working on, and they were consistently accurate in noting what areas they could improve.

Another important teaching skill is being able to recognize individual talents and weaknesses in order to help the learner nurture and improve his/her talents and overcome his/her deficiencies. The teacher must recognize a child's nonverbal expression of how he/she feels about his/her performance and what you believe it should be. I feel deficiencies, as well as talents, need to be recognized in an up-front manner so as to allow the teacher and the learner to first know where the learner is; second, to know where he/she is going; and third, plan how he/she can get there (I can't remember who said it but, "If you don't know where you are going you might end up somewhere else."). The ability of a teacher to recognize individual differences is essential to helping a child set goals. This I found especially important with young children because they lack the experience to know where they should be going and are unaware of how to cultivate their talents leading to success; this is where good adult leadership becomes critical. A good teacher helps the learner develop his/her individual strengths as well as teaches him/her how to become proficient in new areas and in areas in which the learner is weak.

To help the learner develop and grow in skills and in personality, teachers must responsibly assume their role as a positive role model. In my situation this meant setting good examples of sportsmanship toward the other teams and coaches. A teacher must make use of his/her insight to always find something positive in the experience and recognize that every experience serves as a foundation for future learning.

Establishing good rapport with both the learners and their parents is another critical area teachers must work toward. Establishing good rapport with my players was my first objective because I feel that, once established, rapport is the teacher's ticket to motivating and leading learners in a desired direction. Rapport is the cornerstone to effective teaching because it sets the mood of the learning environment. It opens communication lines and communication is essential to teaching/learning. Good rapport gives the teacher a means by which to gain the respect of the learners, which in turn gives rise to the teacher's ability to control and discipline the group or individual if or when necessary.

An important dilemma faced by teachers of young people is that of discipline. How often should I discipline and in what ways? Another dilemma is, "Why should the children listen to me?" Should they believe and follow me just because I am their coach or should they experience the successes for themselves that are made possible by good lessons taught by the teacher? The pace at which to introduce new material is yet another dilemma teachers face. Also, the tendency to favor and give the most attention to the high achievers, the extroverts, and those who show they like you is a constant potential dilemma for teachers.

***Episodes.*** Teaching is by no means a one-way street, and an effective teacher recognizes this. So while a teacher may be motivated and enthusiastic about his/her subject matter, he/she must also consider the motivations of the learners. Does the child want to be where he or she is, or would the child rather be somewhere else doing something else? Does the child participate because he or she has fun and/or wants to learn more to improve his/her skills, or is the child doing an activity to please someone else, like a parent or a federal law (in the case of public schooling)? This is the intrinsic versus extrinsic motivation dilemma. Effective teaching then means stimulating the learner to become curious, eager to find out more, or to learn how something works, or to want to be present in the learning arena. In looking back on my field experience, I recognize that my attitude greatly affected my players' motivation, and this was a very important lesson for me. I looked forward to every Wednesday and Sunday. I always arrived smiling and buzzing with energy; with kids this stuff is contagious. I'd get one kid riled up and excited and it had a domino effect. Within minutes my players were itching to play lacrosse and the stage was set for practice. I constantly ran around and participated in the drills with my players. I would also be sure to pat every child on the helmet or back, shake hands with him or her, and by name ask how life was going. While this may all sound superficial, the group was small enough and the setting appropriate for me to become involved with my players and let them know that I cared about them as individuals and as a team. So far, the parents of three different children and my nephew have told me how much their children look forward to coming to lacrosse practice each week because they have such a great coach and have so much fun. Is there anything more enjoyable and conducive to learning than having fun and liking your teacher? My own educational experience has shown me that I learned best with the teachers I liked the most.

Now that my players were enthusiastic and liked me, the stage was set for teaching effective lessons, and lesson delivery style has multiple possibilities. But I felt it was important to keep my lessons within the reach of my players' demonstrated abilities, teaching them new skills that they could master with time and practice and that would be useful in their repertoire of lacrosse skills. I believe that for a lesson to be effective it must have utility for the learners. For example, a few weeks ago we began to practice taking the ball behind the goal in their offensive end of the field and then looking for a teammate to get open right in front of the goal. As we drilled this tactic the kids seemed to understand it, but I don't think they internalized the tactic or really understood the point of getting the ball behind the goal until our next game, when we scored three goals, including the game winner, using this tactic. After the game one of my players, Paul, came up to me and said, "Coach, how come you didn't show us that before? Look how good it worked." In every game since then, the first thing my players do in the offensive end is get the ball behind the goal.

Because it is rare for any learner to do something purely for personal approval, giving constant positive feedback is another important teaching skill. When I tell my players that they did a good job, I am specific so as to reinforce the desired behavior and let them know that I am really watching over them. In my seventh log entry I noted the importance of feedback. "The children need feedback as they proceed, both to ensure they learn what I want them to learn the way I believe is acceptable, and to let them know what they are doing well and/or poorly and how they can improve."

I believe that without explicit means, such as verbal praise and pats on the back from me as the coach and from their teammates, scoring a goal doesn't mean much (we win competitive sporting events for others, not only ourselves—we feel glory and success because other people praise us; they make us believe we are champions).

As mentioned before, involving the learners in their goal setting and giving them feelings of ownership of their learning direction is a skill teachers must have if they are really interested in the learner's growth. I wasn't so sure giving my players a choice of what to practice was such a good idea, fearing they would fail to recognize their own weaknesses and would choose to practice the drills they were best at, so last week I gave them the reins as an experiment. I questioned them and, WOW, was I surprised that they knew exactly what needed practicing; it was then up to me as teacher to provide them with the exercises/drills to improve on these weaknesses.

I think that the biggest dilemma I faced was that of favoritism. It seems that there is a natural tendency for people to gravitate toward people who are successful and people who like us. Johnny P. is a prime example of success and how he drew my attention. I noted in my fifth log, "He has so much talent it seems unfair not to give him specific attention." It was so easy to like Johnny. He worked hard all through the game, was a very good passer and catcher, was fast, and had a burning desire to improve his play. "He wants to learn more; he knows he can" (Log 5). This I could tell because he always tried out whatever I suggested to him. I found myself overusing Johnny as an example to the other players, potentially putting excessive pressure on him to outperform the others and making the other players envious of my attention toward him. Fortunately, all games had a built-in, fair playing-time mechanism through our system of 3-minute position rotation.

Another dilemma that I and all teachers face is the pace at which new learning material/skills should be introduced. In every teaching situation, time is often the limiting factor. It is difficult to know when your learners have mastered basic skills enough to move on to more complex skills without causing major cognitive confusion or motor skill stifling. Such was the case when I introduced a triangle passing drill to my team. I had to keep the drill in its most elementary form to allow the children to achieve a high level of success and in this way gradually learn the skill. In my seventh journal I wrote, "I kept the drill going in one direction only to facilitate learning, keeping the skill relatively simple." My goal was that my players would learn the basic concepts of lacrosse as precursors to their future success in the game; the educational implication for this is that I believe we learn best from that which we are successful doing (*doing* is a key word here; to really learn something you must, in my opinion, experience it).

Another dilemma I know is frequently faced by teachers is how to discipline or what relationship to establish with the learners—namely, friend, authority figure, or both. Fortunately, discipline was never a problem for me with my team. A warning or command to behave was enough to get them in line. I attribute the lack of disciplinary problems I had to my rapport with my players, their motivation to be at lacrosse practice, and the learning setting in which Marshall Youth Lacrosse is played, that is, if you can't behave or don't like it, you leave.

***Generalizability.***   I wish I could believe that the teaching/learning matrix described in this essay could be taken intact into other contexts, but I'm not that idealistic. However, I do believe that the fundamental elements described for effective teaching, effective lessons, teaching skills, and dilemmas faced by teachers are generalizable to a wide variety of settings that involve groups of young people. Teachers must be able to set achievable goals with their learners and establish an environment conducive to learning. This requires good rapport with both students and parents, overtly recognizing individual differences and cultivating them for the good of the learner, and being a living example and role model for the kids to look to for direction. Also, the learners must have a reason to want to be where they are, in other words, some motivation, which means the teacher should avoid using too many abstract concepts the learners will never use. And finally, the learners should have fun. Learning, although it is often painful as we resolve cognitive dissonance, should be made as enjoyable and pleasurable as possible for all involved. If any of these elements can be achieved by a teacher, a door to learning is opened and a channel for the sharing of knowledge/skills is created.

***Goal Achievement.*** I can honestly say that all of my goals were achieved and that many went well beyond my original expectations. Maybe I underestimated the abilities of my players, but they have improved their passing, catching, and ground ball skills far more than I had anticipated. Being an adult, I guess I had forgotten the rate at which children learn new skills—that is, by leaps and bounds. It is wonderful to watch these children become better lacrosse players and hopefully better people and know that I played a part in this growth.

I feel that I successfully taught a group of twelve 9- to 12-year-olds the important basics of lacrosse. It is really special for me to know that the half of my team who never played lacrosse before are now looking into a future of fun and success as lacrosse players. I am sure that the positive contact my players and I had together will bring them back to lacrosse each spring for many years to come. I was an integral part of a group of young people learning new skills and being turned on to a healthy form of recreation in times when drugs and violence seem to prevail; as a coach I couldn't ask for more.

## NOTE

1. G. J. Posner, *Analyzing the Curriculum* (New York: McGraw-Hill, 1992), p. 85.

# Suggested Reading

Axline, V. *Dibs: In Search of Self.* Boston: Houghton Mifflin, 1964.
A gripping case study of the use of client-centered play therapy in the treatment of one psychologically disturbed young boy.

Ayers, W. *To Teach: The Journey of a Teacher.* New York: Teacher's College Press, 1993.
A beautifully written book in which the author speaks as a teacher, a student, and as a parent.

Berlak, A., and H. Berlak. *Dilemmas of Schooling.* New York: Methuen, 1981.
This book begins with a detailed description of British primary school situations. The authors use this descriptive data to construct a framework for examining schooling, a set of 16 "dilemmas" that all teachers face daily.

Good, T. L., and J. E. Brophy. *Looking in Classrooms.* 6th ed. La Porte, Ind.: Harper-Collins, 1994.
A comprehensive treatment of strategies for observing and describing classroom teaching. A review of classroom research with specific teaching recommendations.

Grant, C., ed. *Preparing for Reflective Teaching.* Boston: Allyn and Bacon, 1984.
A book of thought-provoking readings on teaching. The lead article by Grant and Zeichner is a must.

Jackson, P. W. *Life in Classrooms.* New York: Teacher's College Press, 1968.
An in-depth study of elementary school classrooms. Introduces the concept of the hidden curriculum (see Chapter 5).

Kidder, T. *Among Schoolchildren.* Boston: Houghton Mifflin, 1989.
A beautifully written and sensitive autobiographical case study of an elementary school teacher.

Kowalski, T. J., R. A. Weaver, and K. T. Henson. *Case Studies on Teaching.* New York: Longman, 1990.
A set of brief cases, each introducing a particular issue in teaching.

Lortie, D. *Schoolteacher.* Chicago: University of Chicago Press, 1975.
A classic sociological study of teaching cited in Chapter 5.

Ornstein, A. C. *Teaching: Theory into Practice.* Boston: Allyn and Bacon, 1995.
  An excellent collection of articles on teaching by leading scholars. Includes articles on reflective teaching, multicultural teaching, teaching at-risk students, teachers' perspectives,
  case studies of teaching, classroom management, and classroom observation.

Posner, G. *Course Design,* 4th ed. New York: Longman, 1994.
  A basic how-to-do-it approach to curriculum development.

Posner, G. J. *Analyzing the Curriculum, 2nd ed.* New York: McGraw-Hill, 1994.
  A guide to curriculum study that elaborates the approach used in Chapter 9.

Ryan, K., ed. *The Roller Coaster Year: Essays by and for Beginning Teachers.* New York: Harper-
  Collins, 1992.
  First-year teachers describe the trials and tribulations of the survival year.

Schon, D. *The Reflective Practitioner: How Professionals Think in Action.* New York: Basic
  Books, 1983.
  A thoughtful theoretical treatise on the meaning of reflection for any practioner.

Silverman, R. W., M. Welty, and S. Lyon. *Case Studies for Teacher Problem Solving.* New York:
  McGraw-Hill, 1992.
  Another useful collection of cases for teacher educators.

Sizer, T. R. *Horace's Compromise: The Dilemmas of the American High School.* Boston:
  Houghton Mifflin, 1985.
  One of the most compelling analyses of secondary education in the United States. Of all the
  many current school reform proposals, Sizer's report is the most comprehensive and dis-
  turbing. The readers will have to judge the merits of his recommendations.

Walker, D. *Fundamentals of Curriculum.* New York: Harcourt Brace Jovanovich, 1990.
  A comprehensive, up-to-date, intelligent, and well-written text on curriculum. Chapters 7, 8,
  and 10 are especially relevant to teaching.

Wigginton, E. *Sometimes a Shining Moment.* New York: Doubleday Books, 1985.
  On the one hand, this book represents one educator's perspective on teaching. On the other
  hand, it is the story behind the Foxfire books. An account of a truly courageous and gifted
  teacher's development of an experiential education program that has inspired several hun-
  dred Foxfire-type programs across the United States.

# Index

Activities, assessment of, 74
Adelman, Clem, 99

Bagley, William, 64–65
Behaviorist view, 24
    knowledge, 59
    learning, 51, 52–53
    motivation, 54
Belief inventory. *See* Student Belief
      Inventory; Teacher Belief Inventory
Beliefs. *See also* Perspectives
    analysis of, 80–82
Berlak, Ann, 59–60
Berlak, Harold, 59–60
Brameld, Theodore, 64

Classrooms
    characteristics, 5–6
    informal, 62
    layout, 100–101
Cognitive view, 24
    knowledge, 59
    learning, 52–53
    motivation, 54
Community, analysis of, 92–94
Competition and motivation, 55
Conceptual change philosophy, 58, 59
Concerns, analyzing, 13–15

Conservatives, 64–65
Context
    analyzing concerns about, 14–15
    feature in teaching situation, 5–7
    in field experiences, 11
    and goals, 17
    progress reports, 122
    and significant learning experiences, 37
    social context, 6
    in student-teaching experience, 12
Control, 47–51. *See also* Hidden curriculum
    and conversation with cooperating
      teacher, 114, 116
    and goals, 85
    and perspective, 46, 83
    and Student Belief Inventory, 129–130
    and Teacher Belief Inventory, 81,
      131–132
Conversations, 91
    with cooperating teacher, 113–117
    with principal, 95–96
    with students, 108–109
Cooperating teachers
    conversation with, 113–117
    and goals, 18
    and lesson profile, 104
    relationship with student teacher, 12, 114,
      117